Women in the Vanishing Cloister

Women in the Vanishing Cloister

Organizational Decline in Catholic Religious Orders in the United States

HELEN ROSE FUCHS EBAUGH

Rutgers University Press
New Brunswick, New Jersey

Library of Congress Cataloging-in-Publication Data

Ebaugh, Helen Rose Fuchs, 1942–
    Women in the vanishing cloister : organizational decline in
  Catholic religious orders in the United States / Helen Rose Fuchs Ebaugh.
        p.   cm.
    Includes bibliographical references and index.
    ISBN 0–8135–1865–2 (cloth) — ISBN 0–8135–1866–0 (pbk.)
    1. Monasticism and religious orders for women—United States—
History—20th century. I. Title.
BX4220.U6E33   1993
306.6'559'00973—dc20   92–8035
                                                                CIP

British Cataloging-in-Publication information available

Contents

List of Tables
and Figures

Preface

I begin this book with some fear and trepidation. I am about to sound the death knell for religious orders of women in the United States and argue that they are a dying institution in our society. I feel like the doctor facing the challenge of telling a patient that she has terminal cancer and needs to prepare for the end.

This would be a formidable task if it were not for the inspiration I received in the course of my interviewing with the order that constitutes the case study in this book. By the time I began my formal interviews, the order was well aware that it was in trouble in terms of a declining membership and a high median age of members. I was both amazed and edified at the honesty with which the order was facing its problems. Even though members were talking about the demise of their order, they maintained an optimistic and positive attitude about the order and the richness of life they continued to experience in it. The honesty and courage with which these religious women are accepting their future makes it easier for me to describe the past, present, and future of religious orders as honestly as I can from a sociological perspective.

This book is intended primarily for a sociological audience, most of whom know virtually nothing about Catholic nuns. One reason I am writing the book is to update sociologists on what has happened within religious orders of women in the fifteen years since I wrote *Out of the Cloister* (Ebaugh, 1977). I am constantly taken aback by the stereotypes most sociologists have of nuns, ideas that are at least twenty to twenty-five years outdated. A major purpose of the book, therefore, is to update the sociological literature on religious orders.

Because the book is about an institution in decline, I also hope to contribute to the growing literature on organizational decline. Unlike most declining organizations being studied, religious orders have been around for fifteen centuries and are embedded in the even longer history of the Catholic Church. The fact that this decline in religious orders does not fit the pattern of organizational decline described in the literature raises interesting questions regarding the conditions and responses to decline on the part of different kinds of organizations.

Throughout the book I maintain a sociological perspective. From that stance, the future of religious orders is not very optimistic in terms of its survival. Miracles can happen; however, such happenings are beyond the sociologist's abilities to predict.

I have known many nuns in the course of my life, including my own sister, many teachers and mentors, high school and college friends, as well as colleagues and coworkers. These many and varied associations with nuns over the years have greatly enriched my own life. It is to all these women that I dedicate this book. I want them to know that their lives have touched mine and many lives like mine and that these memories will not vanish, even if the formal institution does vanish in time.

I want to express my appreciation to the Sisters of Service (a pseudonym but they know who they are) for their cooperation with my study. Cooperation is really an understatement, given the warmth and openness with which they shared information with me. I hope that I have been both honest and respectful of the data they shared.

Janet Chafetz, my colleague and friend, has been an integral part of this project, and it probably would not have been done without her support. In addition to critiquing the final manuscript, she originally insisted that the study needed to be done. In addition, she was my sounding board throughout the data collection and analysis stages, and many ideas throughout the book arose during our frequent coffee breaks.

Over the past twenty-five years of our friendship, Jill Alsup and I have discussed many issues that I develop in the book. She also gave her critical eye to the manuscript and made many useful suggestions.

Finally, my husband Albert and my two children, Sarah and Stephen, kept the home fires burning while I was in the field collecting data and became my behind-the-scenes cheerleaders as I wrote the manuscript. In a sense, the final product was a family affair.

Women in the
Vanishing Cloister

CHAPTER 1

Introduction

Religious orders of women are almost as old as the Catholic Church itself. For at least sixteen centuries Roman Catholics have relied upon Catholic nuns not only to provide a model Christian life and Christian education but also to tend the sick, teach the uneducated, and care for the disadvantaged in society. As Catholic immigrant groups came to America they transported both priests to care for their sacramental needs and nuns to teach in their parochial schools and staff their clinics and hospitals. Catholic schools garner respect from educators (see Coleman and Hoffer, 1987) and have survived as a major educational system in our country largely because of the nuns who dedicated their lives to educating youth. Many adult Catholics in the United States have fond memories of their nun-teachers and the sisters in white who ministered to them during hospital stays.

However, the scene is rapidly changing as nuns become "vanishing professionals" (Fichter, 1988) in our society. Their demise is due to the facts that not only has the traditional religious habit been replaced with secular garb but, more important, the number of nuns in the United States has decreased. In 1990 there were 103,269 American nuns—76,685 fewer than in 1965 when the convent population was at its apex. More alarming than the numerical decrease, however, is the fact that few young women are entering religious orders, which has pushed the median age of American nuns to sixty-six years (Wenzel, 1990). With 50 percent of nuns over the age of sixty-six, and virtually no one entering religious orders today, the future of this institution is precarious. It is altogether possible that the presence of nuns in our society is a phenomenon of the past and that the children of the baby-boom generation will grow up with no first-hand knowledge of Catholic nuns.

The demise of the ancient institution of Catholic convents in the United States is the topic of this book. Why is it happening? What factors in both the Church itself and society in general have contributed to the demise? What is happening to convents in the decline process and to the nuns who are aging in a dying institution? Are they demoralized? Why do they opt to remain rather than abandoning the ship? These are some of the questions this book addresses.

Although the book focuses upon religious orders of women in the United States, within the past several decades organizational decline has become a widespread phenomenon in American society as more and more industries and corporations face declining revenues and increased competition. Industry has laid off record numbers of employees in response to recessionary pressures; municipal services have been curtailed as a result of declining revenues; many churches have been forced to close or consolidate owing to financial pressures; schools have had to cut back owing to decreasing enrollments (Whetten, 1980a). The growth and expansion that characterized America in the decades after World War II have given way in the past decade to a situation in which many organizations do not survive. While there were 2.2 million business starts and only 100,000 deaths in the United States between 1950 and 1975 (Statistical Abstract, 1976), the number of business failures more than quadrupled from 1979 to 1985, and the number of new businesses increased by only 25 percent (Cameron et al., 1988).

Religious orders of women in the Catholic Church have followed the pattern of many other organizations in the course of this century. Religious orders in the United States grew dramatically in the decade of the 1950s and into the 1960s and then experienced an equally dramatic decline in the latter half of the 1960s and throughout the 1970s. In fact, between 1950 and 1966, the number of women religious in the United States rose more than 23 percent (from 147,000 to 181,421). From 1966 to 1986 the orders saw their numbers decrease by more than 30 percent (from 181,000 to 126,000), owing to both defections of members and lack of new recruits. As median ages rise in orders and there is little prospect of replacement by new members, it is highly likely that many orders will not survive the present crisis. In fact, as an American institution religious orders may well be in the process of organizational demise and eventual death.

The study of religious orders of women is especially interesting because they have been institutions within the Catholic Church for more than fifteen hundred years. Although their structure and mission have changed over the centuries, there has been continuity in terms of their relationship with the larger Church and their structures of cloister, which isolated members from the larger society. The works and mission of orders were adapted to changing cultural and societal conditions throughout the centuries, but basic continuity existed in organizational form and purpose.

The kinds of changes that have occurred during the past twenty-five years as a response to the Second Vatican Council have resulted in an organizational form that rejects the model of cloister and substitutes identification of members with the outside world. The demise of the cloistered life-style and the inability of contemporary orders to redefine a unique niche in society have led to confusion and anomie among members. In fact, within the past several years, many orders are accepting the possibility of demise as more and more members are questioning the viability of their purpose in postindustrial society. Many orders are shifting their focus from survival to graceful demise.

However, as Rosabeth Moss Kanter and Barry A. Stein maintain, "Organizations rarely die gracefully. There is too much invested in their immortality for people to let go without conflict or tension, or for leaders to be perfectly honest about the possibility of system death" (1979, 373). Sandra Schneiders (1987), in an article widely read by American nuns, states that perhaps the challenge of modern orders is to "die gracefully" as a witness to modern organizations that sometimes organizational demise is necessary.

Organizational Decline

Although some case studies of dying organizations exist (Slote, 1969; Stein, 1979; Loving, 1979), organizational theorists are calling for more detailed studies of the dynamics involved in the decline process, at both the organizational and the individual levels (Cameron et al., 1988; Kanter and Stein, 1979; Kimberley et al., 1980). Researchers agree that the most understudied aspect of the growth and decline process in organizations is organizational death (Sutton, 1984; Whetten, 1980a). The purpose of this book is to fill that gap by documenting organizational decline, and possibly death, in one religious order in the United States.

American culture has traditionally emphasized growth and progress (Whetten, 1980a). Organizational success has been defined in terms of growth. Thus, organizational leaders and managers avoid the subject of decline whenever possible. Terms like decline, retrenchment, cutbacks, and stagnation are replaced by euphemisms like resizing, redesign, and reorganization.

The emphasis on growth is reflected in the organizational literature. Only in the last fifteen years, as organizational growth has given way to more and more organizational decline, has a literature on declining organizations been developed. In fact, approximately 75 percent of the academic literature on organizational decline has appeared since 1978 (Cameron et al., 1988). There have now been sufficient studies of decline to enable one to predict patterns concerning the conditions under which decline occurs, the process of downsizing and retrenchment, and the consequences of decline for both the organization as a unit and the individuals within the organization.

Organizational decline has been defined in various ways, including budget cuts (Behn, 1982), work force reduction (Cornfield, 1983), shrinking revenues (Cameron, 1983), loss of legitimacy (Benson, 1975), and unsatisfactory organizational performance (Hirschman, 1970; Kolarska and Aldrich, 1980). The most comprehensive and empirically relevant definition, however, is that put forth by Cameron et al. (1988) when they define decline as the deterioration of an organization's adaptation to its domain or microniche and, as a result, the reduction of resources within the organization. This definition highlights exchanges between the organization and its environment and the reduction of organizational resources that results from shifts in the organizational-environmental exchange. By focusing the concept of organizational decline upon the lack of adaptation to an environmental niche and the resulting impact upon internal resources, Cameron et al. (1988) provide a more empirically useful approach to the study of decline. Their definition is also more centrally related to the change process that has occurred within religious orders of women during the past two decades because the thrust of change has been adaptation to changing environmental conditions in the last half of the twentieth century.

Structure of Religious Orders
in the Catholic Church

Religious orders exist and are legitimated within the broader system of the Roman Catholic Church. The Congregation for Religious Institutes of Consecrated Life (CICL) is responsible for and coordinates the religious orders of both men and women in the Church. This arm of the Church approves the constitutions of each order and legislates in an ongoing way what is and what is not permitted. In short, the CICL is a Roman office that serves as a control agent in relation to religious orders worldwide.

In terms of finances, ministry, living conditions, and day-to-day operations, each order is administratively independent. The Church, as a formal institution, assumes no financial responsibility for specific orders, a fact made obvious in recent years as more and more orders suffer financial collapse. Statistics on the numbers of religious show that there are 1,190,272 members of religious orders in the world of whom 229,181 are men (including 156,191 clerics and 73,090 lay) and 960,991 women. In the United States there are 151,822 religious members of whom 30,452 are men and 121,370 are women (Schneiders, 1987). There are, therefore, nearly four female religious for every male religious in the world; about one of every seven female religious is American (Schneiders, 1987). These statistics reveal that religious life is overwhelmingly a female phenomenon. It is, therefore, not difficult to see why women religious are the primary change agents in religious life today and why they are frustrated by male clergy's attempts to dictate how change should be effected within their orders.

In its strictest definition, cloister refers to the physical separation of nuns within convents and applies to those religious orders whose members are called contemplative nuns. There are currently some four thousand contemplative nuns in the United States; these women take solemn vows of poverty, celibacy, and obedience, promises lived out primarily through a life of prayer and meditation within the cloister. In contrast, there are currently about five hundred active religious orders in the United States in which approximately 106,000 women take simple vows, which they live out in active ministry in the Church. This book is limited to active religious orders in the United States whose members are technically called *sisters* in contrast to *nuns* in contemplative orders (see Neal, 1990, for further clarification). Given the fact that this book is written primarily for sociologists for whom the distinction is less meaningful, I use nun and sister interchangeably.

Goals of the Book

I have three major purposes in writing this book. First, the process of decline being experienced by religious orders today does not follow the model of decline described in the literature. I propose to describe the ways in which these predictions are not being borne out within religious orders in the United States and to explain why this might be the case. Second, it is my contention that religious orders are caught in an organizational dilemma that will eventually lead to their demise, which they basically have no viable choice in preventing. Given certain exogenous factors, beyond their control, their destiny was established, and their degrees of freedom were limited. These factors include the theological and structural changes set in motion by Vatican II, loss of their unique environmental niche because of changes in Catholic parochial schools in this country, and general societal changes that especially increased opportunities for women. Religious orders had virtually no control over these changes within the larger Catholic Church and within society. Nevertheless, these factors affected changes within religious orders that have had profound consequences for their survival. In the chapters that follow I attempt to demonstrate these organizational dilemmas.

Third, I propose to present an in-depth case study of one order that is experiencing decline. The purpose of the case study is twofold. Primarily I provide sociologists with data on what has occurred in religious orders in the United States in the past twenty years. Few data are available in the sociological literature describing religious orders in the 1980s. Sociologists interested in data on nuns, especially those studying cults, communes, and new religious movements, revert to using outdated case studies such as my book, *Out of the Cloister* (1977), which is based on information collected in the early 1970s. Such far-reaching changes have occurred in religious orders since then that the data are no longer descriptive of the way orders look today.

Furthermore, through the case study I describe in detail the process of organizational decline as it is occurring within one religious order. Although orders differ in specific composition and history, in the past ten years there is greater homogeneity in structure, purpose, and problems than was the case in the decades preceding and immediately after the Second Vatican Council. In fact, there is such homogeneity today that a major issue in religious orders is the definition of what makes one order different from another. As resources diminish, discussions of mergers among orders is becoming one feasible strategy to avert decline.

This book focuses upon religious orders of women in the United States. The extent to which findings can be generalized to orders in other countries is an empirical issue. Even though religious orders worldwide were affected by the events of Vatican II and are responsible to the same Roman authority, the nature and pace at which changes were introduced into orders have varied greatly depending upon societal conditions in individual countries. At points throughout the book, I make predictions about relationships between change in orders and both structural and demographic characteristics of society; however, I do not test these predictions empirically but focus, rather, on changes within orders in the United States.

Organization of the Book

The first three chapters of the book set the scene in terms of placing religious orders in a historical and organizational context. After presenting the overall goals and organization of the book in this first chapter, in chapter 2 I describe the history of religious orders. In chapter 3, I place the decline of religious orders within the larger perspective of organizational decline within profit-making and voluntary organizations. The first part of chapter 4 is a demographic portrait of changes within religious orders in the United States during the past twenty-five years; in the second part of the chapter I introduce the case study order.

Chapters 5 through 10, analyzing the case study order, are organized on the basis of a process model; that is, I present the sequence of factors that influenced the changes in the order. In chapters 5, 6, and 7, I discuss the exogenous factors that set the change process in motion, factors over which the order had little control. Chapter 5 is an analysis of changes in the authority structure in the order; these changes resulted directly from theological shifts mandated by the Second Vatican Council. In chapter 6, I trace the evolution of changes in the occupations of nuns as a result of the changing parochial school system in this country. Chapter 7 focuses upon the drastic decline in the number of new recruits into the order as well as the increase in defections from the order. Both shifts are traced to societal changes, especially the increased opportunities for women. The above changes in the authority structure, in the occupations of nuns, and in recruitment and retention patterns were caused largely by factors outside the control of the order. Whether it was Rome's mandate to change authority, financial problems in the declining Catholic school system, or the expansion of opportunities for women in society, religious orders had little control over these changes. Although the majority of nuns welcomed the changes, religious orders found themselves in the position of adapting to the new ways by effecting structural alterations to accommodate them.

In chapters 8, 9, and 10, I focus upon the structural changes that the religious order made in response to the above exogenous factors. In chapter 8 I focus upon the financial problems that the order faces as a result of a declining membership. Chapter 9 is a discussion of nuns as feminists. I show nuns as both influencing the feminist movement and reacting, in their thoughts and actions, to the effect of the movement. The feminism of American nuns relates directly to the opportunity structures for women in our society.

In chapter 10 I hope to surprise the reader. Given the rather gloomy picture presented throughout the earlier chapters in terms of a declining membership and loss of an environmental niche for religious orders today, one could predict low morale on the part of members in a dying organization. But chapter 10 contradicts this prediction and offers an explanation of why members maintain relatively high morale despite the pessimistic prognosis for their organization.

In chapter 11 I summarize the previous chapters in the light of the predictions from the literature regarding declining organizations. I attempt to explain why religious orders present a deviant case in terms of the predictions. In my effort to summarize the data from previous chapters and to predict the generalizability of the findings I develop a process model of exogenous factors that set in motion the renewal process in religious orders and influenced the ideological and structural changes that eventually lead to their demise. I argue the necessity of testing the model cross-nationally in order to determine the impact of societal factors upon organizational growth or decline. Finally, based on the data from the previous chapters, I return to my argument that religious orders are caught in an organizational dilemma.

CHAPTER 2

From Whence
They Came

To understand the present crisis in religious orders, it is important to know something about the history of religious orders in the Catholic Church. The present crisis is not the first one faced by orders in their fifteen-hundred-year history. I argue, however, that the nature of the challenges being faced today are unique historically and, for the first time, may well result in either the radical transformation of religious orders or, conceivably, even the demise of the institution in the United States. To make this argument cogently, I present a rather detailed history of the evolution and development of religious orders as well as the nature of the previous crises they faced throughout their history.

Religious orders are almost as old as the Catholic Church itself. The first formally structured orders characterized by a distinct, cloistered life-style came into existence in the fifth century, but even during the first four centuries of Christianity women had the option of consecrating themselves to special service in the Church as virgins and widows. There have been variations in the ways in which orders have been structured and in the purposes they have served in the Church over the centuries, yet the fact remains that as an institution it has survived almost fifteen hundred years.

Religious orders have certainly not been static entities during those years. Rather, particular religious orders arose in response to social change in the Church and in the larger social and political institutions in society. Over time, some orders also declined, and many even ceased to exist as new forms began to spring up and flourish. In fact, an analysis of the evolution of orders historically demonstrates the fact that there is a close relationship between major societal shifts and changes in the goals and structures of religious orders in any particular historical era. As Marie Augusta Neal (1990) argues, major structural strains in the institutions of society provide the impetus for widespread changes within religious orders.

The description of the evolution of religious orders, given by Cada et al. (1979) and frequently cited in the literature, is based on the idea of an interactive effect between societal changes and the growth and demise of specific types of religious orders. The following description of the history of religious orders is based on their delineation of five major eras of change summarized in the chart at Figure 2.1.

Ages in the History of Religious Life

The Age of the Desert

In the early centuries of the Church, religious orders did not exist in terms of groups of women who professed celibacy and lived together in a cloistered way of life. Rather, during the early centuries of Christian persecution, the only two clearly defined roles for women in the church were those of virgins and widows. In the writings of St. Paul (1 Timothy 5:3–17) explicit mention is made of these two groups of women who had committed themselves to a celibate way of life "for the sake of the kingdom." A custom grew up in many places of giving those committed to celibacy a special place in Christian gatherings for public worship although they did not yet live in groups but in a secluded way in their own families. By the second century, virgins and widows were clearly distinguished; the former lived, often communally, a secluded existence devoted to prayer and meditation, and the latter engaged in an active mission in the Church.

As the period of persecutions came to an end and the Church began to be officially recognized and accepted in the Roman Empire, a clearly recognizable religious order began to emerge in the form of the holy ascetic who escaped to the desert to pray and do penance. Celibacy came to characterize those who chose this way of life, and gradually the asceticism involved in the renunciation of an active sexual life for the sake of God and His Kingdom came to be seen as a kind of training for martyrdom, a very realistic possibility in the second and third centuries (Schneiders, 1987). This high regard for celibacy and the connection between consecrated nonmarriage and asceticism be-

FIGURE 2.1
Ages in the History of Religious Life

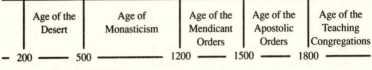

Source: Cada et al., 1979: 13.

came primary characteristics of religious orders, which have continued throughout the history of orders.

Both men and women were attracted to desert asceticism. While many male monks lived solitary lives in the desert, most women lived together in loosely structured communities in which they shared liturgy and prayer. Between 290 and 346 the monk Pachomius and his sister Mary organized several desert monasteries and wrote the first monastic rule. The dominant image of religious life in this period was the holy ascetic who withdrew into the desert to pray, do penance, do battle with the devil, and seek a life of Christian perfection (Cada et al., 1979).

By the fifth century, the golden age of desert monasticism had begun to fade. In the West, the foundations of Roman civilization weakened with the onslaught of barbarian tribes. Monasteries became refugee cloisters where monks gathered the few treasures of civilization. Many monks of this period began to wander from town to town making a nuisance of themselves by their uncouth manners and occasional debaucheries (Cada et al., 1979). The ascetic ideal began to decline and lose its attractiveness. Some religious abandoned their way of life, and fewer people sought to enter desert cloisters. The stage was already being set for the rise of feudal Europe and the next era of the evolution of religious orders. Many patterns that emerged during this first age, however, such as the emphasis upon penance and asceticism as well as celibacy, came to characterize religious orders for the next fifteen hundred years.

The Age of Monasticism

The Age of Monasticism (500–1200 A.D.), often called the classical period of religious orders, can be dated to St. Benedict's founding of the monastery Monte Cassino in 529. Benedict began his religious life as a hermit, but the fame of his sanctity spread so rapidly and widely that many people came to him to be trained in the spiritual life. He accommodated them by setting up monasteries and organizing a form of religious life that soon became dominant in the West; it was considered for many centuries the standard against which any authentic form of religious life was judged (Schneiders, 1987).

As the number of people who came to Benedict seeking instruction increased, he became unable to personally train all of them. He, therefore, appointed spiritual leaders in the form of abbots and abbesses who were in charge of the convents and monasteries. As the West was moving into a system of feudal kingdoms organized around lords and serfs, Benedict established a parallel structure in his monasteries, with the abbot or abbess serving as the feudal lord who protects, cares for, and guides his or her servants as parents would their children. Benedict's conception of the religious community as a family has remained powerful throughout the remaining history of religious orders.

The main work of the monastery was liturgy, which included daily recitation of the Divine Office; that is, psalms were sung at prescribed hours during the day. Study of both religious and classical works was also valued by the monks and nuns. The dominant image of monastic life was the religious engaged in a daily routine of liturgical prayer and contemplation, with attention given to those practical tasks that kept the monastery self-sufficient in terms of basic economic needs.

The monastery became a self-contained local community with an economy that provided everything needed to survive. Monastic living became so successful that the monasteries became wealthy, both intellectually and materially. In fact, the increasing wealth and power of the monasteries brought about a gradual decline in asceticism and fervor and eventually lead to the reform movement within monasteries of the tenth and eleventh centuries. This was the first time in the history of religious orders that reform was considered necessary because orders had fallen away from the rigor and discipline of their initial dedication (Schneiders, 1987).

In general, monastic life was open to women of landed families who believed that having a member in an order of consecrated virgins would bring blessings to both the family and the cities. In addition, because the vow of poverty required of monks and nuns meant the renunciation of inheritance, many large families valued having a son or daughter in the monastery as a way of providing adequate inheritance to the other offspring. In addition, monasteries came to house not only those seeking a religious life but also others—daughters of feudal lords who had no dowries, unfaithful wives put away by their husbands, illegitimate offspring who could not inherit, and women who had lost their families in the various plagues in Europe. Because entering monastic life was often a family, not an individual, decision, subsequent opportunities to relax the rigors of that life were taken by some when they became available. This led to laxity in following the prescribed rule (Neal, 1990).

The eventual decline in the fervor and discipline of the monastery involved abbesses breaking the cloister by going out on the pretense of engaging in business related to the monastery. This was accompanied by other relaxations of the rule such as the wearing of fancy clothes and jewelry, engaging in dancing, going to weddings, neglecting study, avoiding common meals, shirking the common work, and living in separate apartments with servants in attendance (Neal, 1990).

The laxities that crept into monastic life lead to several major reform movements and eventuated in "reformed monasteries," such as Citeaux founded in 1098, the Cistercian monastery at La Trappe, the Camaldolese monastery of Italy, and the Carthusians, founded by St. Bruno in the late eleventh century. The most important reaction to the laxity that had occurred in monasteries, however, came in 1298 in the proclamation of a papal bull entitled *Periculoso* that imposed cloister on religious institutes of women, a restriction in force until the beginning of the twentieth century. The impetus behind the imposition of cloister was twofold: to counteract the laxities that had crept into religious orders, and to provide protection for nuns against the invading barbarians.

By the middle of the twelfth century, various social changes were sweeping Western society, which provoked increased questioning of the meaning and viability of the monastic way of life. Urbanization was emerging with the growth of medieval towns. The Crusades and beginnings of world trade led to greater contact with the Eastern world. The monasteries, with their feudal and cloistered structures, were seen as less and less adequate in meeting both the needs of people raised in this new environment and the needs of the Church as it struggled to evangelize these new lands.

The Age of the Mendicant Orders (1200–1500)

In reaction to the laxities that crept into monasticism, primarily as a result of the wealth that had been accumulated, the next era of religious orders is characterized by a commitment to live in poverty as Christ had done. Begging for alms and wandering from town to town with no permanent residence or worldly goods became the distinguishing feature of religious orders in the thirteenth through sixteenth centuries. Even though monks and nuns in the monastic period renounced individual wealth, over the centuries communal ownership by monastic orders had accumulated to the point of obscuring gospel poverty. The mendicants practiced both communal and individual poverty. Their mobility in moving about the countryside and towns brought the witness of their gospel poverty into the midst of the people. The new mendicant orders that sprung up to train and organize the mendicant friars, such as the Franciscans, Dominicans, and Augustinians existed alongside some traditional cloistered monasteries. Unlike the monasteries, the new mendicant orders experienced dramatic growth within a short time. Within forty years, the Dominicans had a membership of thirteen thousand, and the Franciscans grew even more rapidly (Cada et al., 1979).

Most mendicant orders were established for male religious. It was considered highly improper for women to both live in abject poverty and to wander around begging for alms. However, mendicant orders of men had parallel communities for women members, called "second orders." Although these groups of women shared the same basic spiritual values and image of religious life as their male counterparts, their communities were cloistered, and they were forbidden to live in the poverty offered to men. This was also the era in which "third orders" were founded; namely, these orders had members who made private vows and followed a rule suitable for people living in secular circumstances rather than in convents or monasteries; however, these "third order" members were not recognized as nuns by the Church.

In the Low Countries of Europe the Beguines also arose. Many of the Beguines were women whose husbands were off on the Crusades or had died in the "holy wars." These women chose to live either within communes or in their own homes. They dedicated themselves to a simple, celibate life-style as a means to achieve spirituality through contemplative prayer.

The image of religious life presented by the mendicant orders was that of the simple friar who begs for his keep and follows in the footsteps of Christ. Unencumbered by wealth, the mendicants traveled on foot to any place where they were needed by the Church and were ready to preach, cultivate learning, serve the poor, and minister to the needs of society in the name of the Church (Cada et al., 1979).

Paradoxically, by the late fourteenth and early fifteenth centuries, the mendicant orders that had been founded to counteract the laxities of wealth in the monasteries succumbed to the same evils. Because their rule forbade laymen to pass through their front entrances, in a legalistic manner, the friars and nuns built rear entrances so that cooks and servants could enter to prepare meals and provide for their comfort. Seamstresses and tailors were invited in to sew garments for the monks and nuns and sometimes lingered for amorous encounters.

Midway through the fourteenth century, religious orders were ravished by the Black Death plague that hit Europe. Large numbers of religious died, especially the more devout who went into the towns to care for the people afflicted by the disease.

As the Renaissance brought a new humanism and secularization to European society and as the Reformation was challenging the legitimacy of the Catholic Church, the traditional forms of both monastic and mendicant orders came into question. Once again it seemed that the stage was set for a new era of religious orders.

The Age of the Apostolic Orders (1500–1800)

By the middle of the fifteenth century far-reaching changes were transforming European society. The new humanism of the Renaissance laid the groundwork for the rationality that was to characterize the next few centuries of European thought. Printing, a novel invention, was making learning available to more people. There was an atmosphere of optimism about human potential. Even a new world had been discovered in America. In contrast, the laxity of religious orders, as well as of the entire church in the Middle Ages was challenged by Luther's Protestant Revolt, which virtually eliminated religious orders in those countries that became Protestant (Cada et al., 1979).

The two major responses to the decline of religious orders at this time were represented by the founding of the Jesuits for men and the

Ursulines for women, both with the goal of providing an elite corps of dedicated servants ready to aid the Church in its new apostolic needs of the Counter-Reformation. Both groups valued a high level of personal holiness that would enable the religious to face the new tasks of the Church without all the protections of the monastery.

Among the women religious, the Ursulines, founded by Angela Merici, exemplified the new thrust of religious life. Originally the nuns lived in their homes and formed a loose-knit company of virgins devoted to assisting the poor and caring for the infirm. Shortly after the foundress's death, the group was forced to comply with the new decrees of the Council of Trent (1545–1563) that reaffirmed that all nuns must be cloistered or suffer excommunication from the Church. Gradually the group acquiesced and became cloistered nuns. Other orders, such as the Visitation nuns founded by Francis de Sales, the Daughters of Charity, and the St. Joseph Sisters, succeeded in being apostolic and evading the cloister, probably because their small size made them inconspicuous to Church authorities (Neal, 1990). Although these orders set a precedent in terms of apostolic service, they never received the formal approval of Church authorities and were not recognized as religious orders until the twentieth century. Many structures of physical isolation were relaxed in these apostolic orders, but they continued to maintain less obvious structures of cloister such as celibacy, recitation of the Divine Office throughout the day, identification and socializing with other nuns, and a form of asceticism that distanced them from worldly concerns.

By the eighteenth century religious orders had nearly died out in Europe as the Enlightenment undermined the rationale for religious life. The Jesuits were suppressed in 1773, and many orders simply passed out of existence either by state suppression or departure of members.

The Age of the Teaching Congregations (1800–present)

In the course of the nineteenth century a new flourishing of orders was evident throughout Europe. About six hundred new religious orders were founded during that century. These orders were dedicated to building and staffing various types of parochial institutions such as schools, hospitals, and agencies to assist the poor and needy. The orders were committed to having their members selflessly apply themselves to attaining the professional standards required to operate these institutions. Members in these orders sought to dedicate their lives to the salvation of their own souls and to the salvation of others by blending an intense pursuit of personal holiness with a highly active apostolic service (Cada et al., 1979).

As education of the masses became a goal for the industrialized world, religious orders became involved in teaching with the hope of providing a religious education along with secular learning. They attempted to reach large numbers of Catholics and potential Catholics and to teach them Christianity by using the institutions emerging in modern society. Unlike in earlier centuries the Jesuits' goal of influencing noblemen through education, the goal of religious orders in the nineteenth and twentieth centuries was to reach the masses. Now religious women took the lead in providing both religious and secular education to as many people as possible.

Many of these new religious orders of women saw the cloister as an impediment to their apostolic work. They, therefore, established rules that allowed the nuns to leave the convent for periods of time in order to engage in active work outside the cloister; however, the rule required that they return to the convent after their work was done to share in liturgy, prayer, recreation, and meals. The elimination of the physical cloister was seen as so radical by Church authorities that these women were not allowed to make permanent, solemn vows but only yearly renewals. Their way of life was seen as something less than the authentic consecrated life (Neal, 1990). Not until 1900 were these apostolic orders recognized in the canons of the Church as true religious congregations.

During the years from 1600 to 1950, the Church made periodic efforts through canonical pronouncements to enforce the restrictions of the cloister on religious women. The Church insisted that nuns wear religious garb, including the veil, that they travel in pairs, that every convent require the recitation of the liturgical office, and that members pray in common.

By 1950 the demand for nuns to staff schools, hospitals, and social service centers put a strain on religious orders in terms of providing both the numbers of personnel needed and the kinds of credentials required by state and private agencies. Professionalization, becoming an important value in secular society, had far-reaching consequences for what was soon to happen in religious orders. Already, in 1929, Pope Pius XI in his encyclical, *The Christian Education of Youth*, encouraged nuns to obtain the education and experience necessary to staff these institutions. In the twenty years after the encyclical, nuns began to obtain professional education by attending universities, usually Catholic ones, on weekends and during the summer. Given the demands of their religious profession in terms of prayer and meditation within the cloister, many nuns began to feel overburdened (Meyers, 1965).

In the early 1950s, Pope Pius XII became very concerned with the fact that many nuns who staffed Catholic institutions were inadequately trained professionally. He felt that an injustice was being done to the people being served by religious who did not have the necessary credentials for their work. He called an International Congress of superior generals in Rome and encouraged these leaders to train their nuns professionally on a par with their secular counterparts in their various professional settings (Ebaugh, 1977). Inspired by this encouragement from the pope, many superior generals from the United States began sending nuns to all kinds of educational and professional schools, secular as well as Catholic. In the decades of the 1950s and 1960s, educational levels of American nuns rose dramatically and continued to rise for the next several decades. For example, in 1966 68 percent of religious women in the United States had a college education; by 1980 that number had risen to 88 percent, with 68 percent having advanced degrees (Neal, 1984).

Spurred on by the pressures for higher education and the fact that nuns from different congregations found themselves living together in convents near universities, the Sister Formation Conference was established in 1954 to develop a program for training new members; the system combined professional training with religious formation. Part of the work of this new conference was developing a theology and spirituality that would motivate young women to take on a life of celibacy for the purpose of serving God and the Church in an apostolic calling. Through a highly organized series of workshops, retreats, and published materials, the Sister Formation Conference, along with the newly organized Conference of Major Superiors of Religious Congregations of Women (CMSW), developed and disseminated a new conception of the mission of religious orders. This new conception called for vowed poverty as a way of witnessing and serving the needy in society, celibacy as greater freedom of time and energies to serve those in need, and obedience to the mission of the Church as expressed in the gospels (Neal, 1990). This new approach did not initially deny the value of a semi-cloistered way of life for religious women; however, greater emphasis began to be placed on the value of witness and availability to the people being served within the institutions in which nuns worked.

Contemporary Religious Orders

By the time of the Second Vatican Council (1962–1965) far-reaching changes in theology and a sense of mission had occurred within religious orders of women. Lacking, however, were the types of structural changes needed to accompany the shifts that had taken place in ideology and the sense of purpose and meaning for religious orders in the twentieth century. As a result, many nuns were feeling the strain and anomie created by the juxtaposition of new ways of viewing religious life hampered by outdated structures that made it difficult to live out a new mission within a cloistered life-style.

As a result of the education movement among nuns, a more widely informed audience of nuns eagerly awaited the renewal and change initiated by the Second Vatican Council in its document, "Decree on the Appropriate Renewal of Religious Life." Its basic directive is summarized in an opening paragraph: "The appropriate renewal of religious life involves two simultaneous processes: (1) a continuous return to the sources of all Christian life and to the original inspiration behind a given community; and (2) an adjustment of the community to the changed conditions of the time" (Abbott, 1966). Every order was mandated to analyze its goals and structures in the light of these two goals and to effect the necessary changes in its formal constitutions. Change, therefore, was not only encouraged by the Council but also mandated. Each order was instructed to reevaluate its life-style and structure, experiment with renewed forms, and eventually submit a new constitution to Rome for approval.

In addition, the decree and later instructions from Rome mandated that every nun should take part in examining and reorganizing religious life according to the principles set forth in the decree. Leadership in the order was not to impose change, but reformation was to proceed democratically with the involvement of the entire membership. "Renewal Chapters" were to be set up on the basis of elected delegates from the membership. By the time the decree was issued, many orders had in their membership women with advanced degrees and training in various disciplines. Not only theological expertise was brought to bear in implementing the council decree but also insights from history, sociology, psychology, economics, social work, and almost every other discipline imaginable. Thus, an educated group of nuns set about to restructure religious life to meet the needs of contemporary society.

Although many specific changes were effected in religious orders as a result of the renewal and adaptation process, these changes can be summarized as a process of dismantling the traditional cloister of the convent and substituting structures that emphasized greater identification with the laity in the Church. In fact, the council fathers themselves set the agenda by insisting that nuns were not clerics but laity who dedicated their lives to special witness of the gospel. With this in mind, nuns set about to restructure their life-style in a way that allowed greater participation with the laity.

Even though apostolic communities had been in existence at least 450 years, the cloistered life had remained characteristic of religious orders of women. Nuns in the twentieth century were allowed to leave the convent for specified periods of time to do their apostolic works; however, they were to espouse a set-apart, cloistered, spiritual mentality even in the midst of their work, and they were to return to the cloister immediately upon completing their apostolic duties in order to reestablish and nourish their spiritual life. For fifteen hundred years, nuns were cloistered not only physically but also socially; social restrictions kept them separated from "outsiders" and focused upon a communal life oriented to prayer and penance. Precisely these structures of cloister came under scrutiny as religious orders began the process of adaptation to modern society. In almost every aspect of life-style, structures of cloister gave way to changes that promoted less separation from society and more openness and involvement with people outside the cloister. The following examples describe the kinds of changes effected by most orders in the years following the Council. Even though each order reevaluated its own structures, in terms of the general character of religious life the result was similar. Although some variations existed, especially in the decade of the 1970s as orders implemented their changes at different rates and times, religious orders are once again appearing more and more homogeneous.

Dress

One of the first outward manifestations of change in nuns after the Council was the modification of the religious garb that historically set nuns apart from the rest of society. The rationale behind the change in religious garb was that the habit hindered the ability of the nun to establish rapport and a sense of identification with those to whom she ministered. Moreover, the religious habit, as it was called, originated in earlier centuries as the simple garb worn by peasant women. Paradoxically, over the centuries, what was once a way of identifying with the masses became a symbol of remoteness and differentiation. In an attempt to remove what nuns saw as a barrier to association with the laity, most religious orders at first modified the habit to a simple suit and veil and then eventually allowed their members to wear whatever simple clothing they desired. While some orders still encourage their members to wear a symbol of their dedicated life, such as a ring or a cross, many nuns today are totally unidentifiable as members of religious orders.

Housing

For centuries, nuns have lived communally under the authority of an abbess or superior, usually in large convent buildings that accommodated all members of an order. These "motherhouses" became symbolic of the order. Even when local communities were formed in which smaller groups of nuns lived together under a local superior, in some orders the entire membership came together at the motherhouse for a period of time, such as several weeks during the summer months.

Each motherhouse was set apart from the surrounding neighborhood by walls, grounds, or mammoth structures of the convent itself. Outsiders were sometimes permitted within the convent walls, but each motherhouse had "cloistered" rooms or areas, off limits to anyone who was not a member of the order.

In the process of renewal, religious orders abandoned cloistered areas and opened their doors to visitors. Today, many convent structures are being transformed into nursing homes, retreat centers for the laity, and even civic centers.

Although the "local community" still exists in the form of five to six nuns living together, in most instances there is no superior. This form of life-style has also become only one of many living options for nuns. Even more common in many orders is the individual nun living alone in a house or apartment or, in some instances, with one or two other nuns of her own or another order. Usually, each nun has a different job, is assigned the use of a car, has an individual budget, and often her own circle of friends. In most orders the individual decides which living situation she prefers. Usually there is no local superior; rather, the nun is responsible, in a very general sense, to a "regional superior" or "contact person" who is a kind of liaison between the central administration of the order and the individual nuns.

Exposure to Media

Until the 1960s nuns were cloistered from all types of media sources that would expose them to the outside world. Newspapers and magazines were forbidden in many convents. Even after the advent of television, there were few television sets in convents. On rare occasions a superior might bring in a radio or a television and allow the nuns to listen to a selected program, but in general nuns were isolated from the events and influences of the broader world.

The goal that motivated isolation from the events of the world was to minimize distractions that would interfere with the nun's total concentration on the kingdom of God. As that kingdom became increasingly identified by Vatican II as a "kingdom on earth," and as the Council leaders moved away from the ghetto mentality of the Church (Sweeney, 1980) to an emphasis upon Christian involvement in the world, the convent rules regarding exposure to the media shifted. In fact, knowledge of what was going on in world events became positively valued as religious orders began to see their mission as intimately tied into the creation of God's kingdom on this earth.

Social Relationships

Physical isolation is one structure groups use to separate members from outside influences. Another important way to achieve separation is the creation of social isolation—that is, the manipulation of members' social ties and associations with outsiders. Structures of social isolation affect the reference groups with which members compare themselves. By assuring that members associate only or primarily with other groups members, orders reduced the possibility of rival threats to loyalty.

As I argue in an earlier book (Ebaugh, 1977), change in the rules regarding social isolation was one of the most profound shifts made by religious orders following Vatican II. From a sociological perspective, social isolation is more central to the notion of cloister than physical isolation because social ties affect members' reference groups and, ultimately, the degree of commitment that members maintain to the group. As nuns were sent to universities, both Catholic and secular, to improve their professional competencies, they came into contact with lay men and women who provided alternative life-style models. In many cases, the nuns began to shift their reference group orientation away from a celibate, religious life to that of either a single or married life in secular society. Data show that as education levels rose in religious orders so did rates of membership exit (Ebaugh, 1977).

In pre–Vatican II religious orders numerous structures assured the social isolation of members. Nuns seldom went outside the convent alone but rather in the company of other nuns. Such necessary excursions as visits to the doctor's office, dentist appointments, and necessary shopping were done with other nuns. Nuns usually received visitors in the presence of at least one other group member. This rule applied even to parents and other family members. Every five or six years nuns were allowed to visit their families in their hometown; however, they were not allowed to spend the night in their parents' home but had to return to the local convent to sleep. During the day, a fellow nun went with them to visit family. As a result of these rules, nuns were seldom in situations in which they had no social support from group members. Rather, the group, with its distinctive norms and values, was always present to counteract any outside pressures, direct or indirect. Consensual validation, in the form of social support for ideas, convictions, and commitments, was ever present for the traditional nun.

In many convents, incoming and outgoing mail was read and distributed at the discretion of the superior. Telephone calls were received by the superior who judged whether the individual nun should be allowed to receive them. Outgoing calls and visits to the parlor required permission.

Proscriptions against association with outsiders made up just one facet of social isolation. Equally important were the structures that encouraged close primary ties with fellow nuns. The daily life of the convent followed very closely Goffman's (1961) description of a total institution in which large numbers of like-situated individuals, cut off from the wider society, live, work, eat, sleep, and recreate together. Individuality is deemphasized by uniformity in dress, personal belongings, furniture, and daily schedule. Clear distinctions are made between subordinates and superiors.

Unlike most of the total institutions Goffman (1961) discusses, religious orders differ in that voluntary membership is based on consensual validation rather than force. During the 1950s and early 1960s when orders experienced great growth, it was not unusual for an order to admit between 50 and 100 new members in a given year. New recruits entered during or immediately after high school and were told that they were responding to a special call or vocation from God. The fact that so many others were also responding to the call and accepting the instruction and rules being imposed by superiors gave credence to the life-style. Consensual validation made it easier to conform than to deviate, and most new members came to accept the total way of life in the convent as God's call for them.

In the past twenty years many traditional structures of religious orders have changed as fewer recruits entered and the effects of Vatican II were implemented. In many ways convent life today hardly resembles the life of nuns prior to the Council. Despite changes in religious orders over the centuries, pre–Vatican II orders maintained two constants: (1) a celibate way of life, and (2) the cloister in terms of physical and social separation from mainstream society. In post–Vatican II orders, the commitment to a celibate life remains, even though theological interpretations of the meaning and functions of celibacy have changed. The structures of cloister, however, have undergone the most drastic changes since the Council. For this reason, along with changing opportunity structures for women in the last half of the twentieth century, I argue that religious orders of women in the United States are on the decline in a way that has not characterized prior eras. Although it is possible that forms of religious life will survive in a revitalization process, it seems highly unlikely that these forms will be built upon the basis of separation from the world.

The Vatican Council itself rejected the century-old siege mentality of the Church (Seidler and Meyer, 1989), legitimized by Vatican I in 1870, and substituted an attitude of involvement in the world. Vatican II declared that solidarity with all people of the world was the vocation of the Christian. The basis of renewal for religious orders, as outlined in the Council's document on religious life, was the renewal and adaptation of structures to the original inspiration of Scripture and to the changed conditions of the times. Throughout the decree, religious orders were encouraged to review every aspect of their life-style in light of modern society and to effect those changes that would bring the order into the modern century. The basis of the renewal that orders underwent in the ten years after the Council was to disassemble those rules and regulations that created distance and separation from the world and to substitute structures that immersed nuns in the midst of the world. As a result, precisely the cloister, with all of its physical and social implications, was discarded and replaced with a life-style centered in the midst of mainstream society. This loss of cloister distinguishes the current changes in religious orders from the eras of change that had occurred previously.

The demise of the structures of the cloister, however, has been accompanied in most orders by a sense of anomie in terms of the purpose or mission of religious orders in the contemporary world. The fact that nuns are now defined as Christians witnessing to the kingdom of God in the world does not differentiate them theologically from the role that noncelibate laity have by virtue of their baptism. As nuns engage in varied types of careers, live singly or in small groups in homes or apartments, associate with noncelibate lay men and women, and have greater freedom in their everyday lives, many nuns have come to question what distinguishes them from other laity in the Church. In my earlier study of ex-nuns (Ebaugh, 1977) I found that many who had left religious life in the early 1970s felt that the costs of celibacy were no longer balanced by the types of rewards that were previously associated with religious life. In traditional religious life, the nun held high status in the Church and was esteemed by the laity as set apart for special service for God and the Church. She was considered a "holy person" with special gifts and access to the spiritual realm. The "holy habit" and cloistered way of life reinforced the sense of awe and mystery in which laity, Catholic and nonCatholic alike, held the nun. As this mystery disappeared after Vatican II and nuns became more like other laity, the special esteem in which they were held faded. Thus, many nuns reevaluated the unique role religious women play in the modern Church.

The anomie that many nuns felt in terms of role and mission gradually generalized to orders as a whole so that today the major question most orders face is that of their mission in the Church. Because orders are no longer committed to specific works—teaching, hospital work, or social services—they face the issue of what makes them unique in the Church.

In addition to the demise of the structures of cloister that has occurred since Vatican II, a second reason I argue that the current changes in religious orders are substantially different from those that occurred in previous centuries relates to changes in society regarding career and life-style opportunities for women in general. In most societies, until the middle of the twentieth century women had few career options other than marriage and domestic tasks. The women who worked outside their own homes found jobs as domestic servants or in domestic-related businesses such as tailoring, bakeries, or schools. Even more common in the early industrial era, women engaged in home industries such as running boardinghouses, taking in laundry and sewing, and working in home industries on a piecework basis or finding jobs in factories and sweatshops. With the rise of large corporations, the expansion of the economy, bigger government, accelerated urbanization, and advanced transportation and communication of the late nineteenth century, more and more women began to enter the paid labor force in the Western industrialized countries (Anderson, 1988). In the United States, for example, the percentage of females in the labor force rose from 18.2 percent in 1890 to 54.5 percent in 1985 (U.S. Bureau of the Census, 1975, 1986). However, until the past two decades or so women, even educated ones, tended to be employed in lower paid, less prestigious jobs such as clerical and sales work. Only during the last two or three decades have career opportunities gradually expanded for younger, college-educated women. The trend toward more women in the professions is evident in the numbers of women students admitted into medical and law schools today where often more than half of a graduating class is female compared with minuscule percentages just ten to fifteen years ago (Anderson, 1988).

In addition to professional careers opening up to women in the latter half of the twentieth century, life-style options are also greater for women today than they were in previous eras. The stereotype of the single female as old maid or spinster has changed as more and more women opt to remain single and/or childfree for various reasons or to postpone marriage and children until their late twenties or thirties.

The options for a life of commitment to Church and religion are also greater than ever for both Catholic men and women as laity become more and more involved on parish and diocesan levels. In fact, even full-time positions traditionally held by priests and nuns—coordinator of religious education, principal of parochial schools, and adult education coordinator—are increasingly held by lay people as the numbers of clerics and religious diminish. Even the newest role of administrator of parishes is becoming a possibility for married women as well as nuns (Wallace, 1992). Unlike previous eras in the Church, becoming a nun is no longer the only option for Catholic women who want to devote themselves to serving the Church in a special way.

It is also the case that many nuns today are resenting and challenging what they see as male dominance in the Church. A constant issue of debate within religious orders is whether to comply with objections from Rome regarding the revised constitutions that orders are required to submit or to ignore formal (canonical) approval of an agency comprised almost exclusively of men and continue the kinds of policies judged appropriate by the order. To refuse to comply means that the order would lose "canonical status" in the Church; that is, it would not be formally recognized as a religious order. This change in status is important to some members of every order (often the older nuns) but less important to others. As a result, conflict often arises regarding the merit of official approval.

In fact, one of the fastest growing types of religious life today are the noncanonical communities of women. More than four hundred such groups exist (Schneiders, 1987). Members in these communities make private vows of celibacy, poverty, and obedience and devote themselves completely to ministry in the Church. Their noncanonical status protects them from surveillance and control from the Vatican without limiting their ability to minister. While they are not recognized as religious orders by Rome, little in terms of mission and life-style differentiates them from members of officially recognized orders. The freedom from official approbation by the Vatican protects these groups from neither the dilemma of defining a unique mission in the Church nor the competing opportunities for young women in today's world. Many members in these noncanonical orders are defectors from canonical orders, women who refused to stay in orders that are under the domination of Rome. It remains to be seen how many new members will be recruited from young Catholic women who have never been part of a religious order.

In summary, the change occurring in religious orders of women today is substantially different from the changes that have occurred periodically in the previous fifteen-hundred-year history of orders. For the first time, the major focus of change is the elimination of all the structures of cloister and isolation from the world and the substitution of both a theology and life-style that stresses presence and identification with the world. In addition, cultural and social changes have provided more opportunities for women in terms of both careers and life-styles. As a result of these changes, it is highly likely that religious orders as we have known them for fifteen hundred years in the Catholic Church will not survive their current crises.

CHAPTER 3

Organizational Decline

The literature on organizational decline makes it clear that patterns emerge in organizations as they face declining resources and issues of survival. Among the most common effects of decline are centralization of authority, internal reallocation of resources, manipulation of the environment, internal discord leading to turf battles, and finally, increased loss of morale and increased cynicism among members. In this chapter I discuss each of these consequences, show how the decline in religious orders has not followed the predicted patterns, and discuss reasons why religious orders constitute a deviant case.

Centralization of Authority

As organizations begin to decline, authority tends to become more centralized and less participative (Staw et al., 1981; Cameron et al., 1988; Smart and Vertinsky, 1977; Bozeman and Slusher, 1979; Whetten, 1980a). As Levine (1979) points out, leaders are usually aware that participation facilitates change; however, leaders also know that participation in their own demise is not a viable process for members and often leads to conflict. In an effort to avoid conflict and keep members content, leaders tend to make the tough decisions themselves and inform members after the fact (Yetten, 1975).

When resources are scarce, which they frequently are in decline situations, mistakes become more visible and costly, and administrators want to take neither the time nor the risks involved in consulting members. As a result of centralization, communication channels are restricted, a situation that increases the likelihood leaders will be blamed for mistakes by members who feel uninformed. Leadership credibility suffers, which often leads to high turnover (Whetten, 1980b; Greenhalgh and Rosenblatt, 1984; Levine, 1979).

Because decline is threatening to leaders and produces stress, there is a tendency toward rigidity among leaders (Staw et al., 1981). It is easier to define situations in terms of existing programs for dealing with problems and avoiding the additional stress that innovation often produces. Tunnel vision results where leaders define situations in terms of existing programs and are unwilling to consider novel solutions.

Likewise, leaders of declining organizations are likely to show a preference for quick response to relieve the tension that decline produces; this often precludes the careful diagnosis essential for adequate solutions (Whetten, 1980a). Stress also tends to foster "problemistic search" in which solutions are sought for the symptoms rather than for more systemic change (Cyert and March, 1963; Smart and Vertinsky, 1977). Often during decline the resources are also lacking for planning, consultation, and information that might minimize the tunnel vision of leaders.

Change can also be threatening for administrators who face either a possible loss of their jobs or a reduction of their responsibilities and status in the event of radical system change. As Michels (1949) pointed out, conservative oligarchies tend to form within organizations, and, over time, these oligarchies become increasingly protective of their self-interests.

Unlike what is predicted in the literature for declining organizations, within the past twenty-five years authority within religious orders has become increasingly more democratic and participative. The hierarchical structure of authority from the superior general and her council to local superiors has been replaced by representative groups composed of elected members, committees, regional coordinators, and general assemblies of the membership. Although the superior general (now often called president) and her elected council of advisers may retain the legal authority for corporate actions, it has become both policy and accepted practice in most orders for decisions to be made in a collegial manner.

In fact, decentralization of authority and participatory democracy on the part of the membership are major characteristics of the changes that have occurred within religious orders since Vatican II. In both the Council document on religious orders ("Decree on the Appropriate Renewal of Religious Life," 1965) and the document on implementation (*Ecclesiae Sanctae*) issued by Pope Paul VI in 1966, orders were encouraged to involve every member in its reevaluation and implementation of renewal. The shift from centralization of authority to participatory democracy resulted from the deliberations of the renewal process.

Twenty-five years ago religious orders exemplified an authoritarian, totalistic institution; today they more closely resemble a voluntary organization in which members join together because of common interests and purposes (Ebaugh, 1977). Like many voluntary associations, members elect a president and board of directors who coordinate activities of the group. Gone is any notion of the divinely conferred "grace of office" that authorized previous administrators with the right to administer and required of members the duty to obey. Along with both decentralization of authority in religious orders during the past several decades and the increased utilization of a committee structure has been an increase in the dissemination of information regarding the operations of the organization. Some orders convene a general assembly of all members at least once a year. These assemblies inform members of the current state of the organization and develop policies. In addition to the annual general meetings, most orders have a structure that brings members together during the year in smaller, usually regional, groups to keep abreast of issues. Because a representative of the administration is usually present at these meetings, they dispel rumors and assure that communication takes place between the administration and the membership. In addition, routine newsletters report ongoing activities of both the administration and the membership.

Internal Allocation of Resources

As organizations begin to decline, there is a tendency to allocate increasing resources to internal functions as a way of analyzing and ameliorating the decline process. Tsouderos's (1955) study of ten voluntary organizations shows that administrative expenditures and number of office workers increase rapidly after the downturn toward shrinkage. Freeman and Hannan (1975) analyzed changes in numbers of administrative personnel in 805 school districts in California and found that administrative components grew as districts shrunk in numbers of students.

As organizational leadership realizes that resources are decreasing and that the organization is losing its niche in its environment, there is a tendency to try to solve the problems by hiring consultants to analyze what is wrong, allocating more internal positions such as recruiter, financial analyst, development officer, and market analyst, and intensifying administrative positions to "turn the organization around."

As religious orders have begun to decline in the past fifteen years, they have opted to reduce internal positions and allocate increasing resources to external goals. Most notably, in line with their ideological stance of "opting for the poor," many orders have encouraged their members to take jobs working with the poor, jobs that frequently provide very low pay and poor benefits. As a result, the order has to subsidize these members from its general fund, a practice that has contributed to the severe financial crisis in most orders today. Likewise, many orders are committing resources toward efforts to effect systemic changes in society that would empower the poor, the oppressed, and the marginalized. Wittberg (1988) found in her analysis of congregational documents that 75 percent of religious orders maintain identification with the poor as a primary goal of the order.

During the same period that orders have focused upon service to the poor and risk taking, there has also been a corresponding deemphasis upon internal concerns such as membership recruitment and maintaining a unique group identity (Kolmer, 1984; Wittberg, 1988). As a consequence, their outward focus and willingness to risk may, in the long run, be dysfunctional for the orders. As Kanter (1972) shows, no communal group in her study that began to ignore membership recruitment and boundary maintenance survived beyond a generation.

Fear of Risk Taking

The onset of decline tends to inhibit creativity and risk taking (Schuler, 1980; Staw et al., 1981; Smart and Vertinsky, 1977; Bozeman and Slusher, 1978). Frequently, membership in declining organizations tends to become more homogeneous as the more creative risk takers among the membership tend to be the first to leave (Greenhalgh, 1983; Argenti, 1976; Hirschman, 1970). It also becomes more difficult to recruit creative members into an organization that is shrinking rather than growing. The administration's preoccupation with greater efficiency in running the organization leads to increased control, standardization, and streamlining programs. This stance tends to further alienate the more creative risk takers among the members and leads to the loss of these people.

Reduced experimentation in terms of goals and programs tends to set in as leaders struggle to maintain the status quo rather than risk loss of resources to new programs. As Whetten (1980a) demonstrates, decline increases the pressure of accountability such that leaders are likely to pursue courses of action with immediately visible and measurable consequences. Under conditions of decline and threat to survival, efficiency is emphasized as both a resource-saving strategy and a way to assure members that effective changes are being made.

During decline, organizations frequently lack the resources, both financial capital and workforce, to introduce and develop new programs. All changes in routine demand start-up costs. The declining organization may not be able to effect significant changes, even though they may be needed.

Rather than fear of risk taking, religious orders have abandoned their secure positions in all types of settings in favor of greater diversity, in not only occupational terms but also life-style of members, financial arrangements, and systems of accountability. In fact, experimentation has been the organizational stance of orders since the Council.

As Wittberg (1988) argues, based on her analysis of congregational administrative reports and chapter documents, religious orders in the past two decades have shown a willingness to experiment with all types of new ministries. Even with fewer members and declining resources, they have gradually moved away from traditional institutional commitments (Kolmer, 1984; Neal, 1984). Concomitantly, rather than assigning members to specific jobs in these institutions, orders today allow significantly more individual choice in the selection of jobs. In fact, in most contemporary orders, the nuns themselves have the responsibility of finding suitable jobs rather than being assigned by the administration to fill specific institutional positions. This change in practice has resulted in a much greater diversity among occupational commitments. Because most orders have professed a commitment to the poor, many jobs that nuns are selecting are low paying jobs in both the public and private sectors. As a result, orders must subsidize the living expenses of these members; a major issue in many orders today, as they face increasing financial problems, is the number of such sub-sidized positions an order can support.

As orders allow more individual choice in both job procurement and living situation, they face the risk of reduced control over members. Many nuns are both working and living in situations in which there are no other nuns. The consensual validation and mutual support that was ever-present in traditional orders is no longer the taken-for-granted life-style of nuns. By permitting such diversity, religious orders risk the challenges of outside influences. Orders have opted for greater individualism rather than a totalistic, authoritarian system even though the risks of defection and lessened commitment to the group are greater.

Intraorganizational Turf Battles

Conditions of decline inherently involve restricted resources and pressures to retrench. Levine (1978, 1979), Whetten (1980a), and others have noted the intensification of conflict under these conditions as fights over a smaller resource base and consequent attempts to protect turf predominate. As resources decline in organizations, interest groups tend to form within the organization as a means of assuring that they will receive their fair share of the pie. The relationship between interest groups is inevitably conflictual (Dahrendorf, 1959) because resources are limited. Adaptation means change, which has different consequences for the various interest groups. The administration can hardly afford resistance to innovation. And, yet, the failure to adapt frustrates and angers other groups within the organization. Because of the scarcity of resources, the administration often cannot afford increased side payments to disadvantaged groups. Adaptation may therefore be too costly to the organization (Greenhalgh, 1983).

Turf battles in religious orders have tended to focus not on the allocation of resources to specific works or groups in the organization but on conflicts between those groups advocating change, modernization, and democratization within the order and those resistant to the renewal process. In many instances these battles tend to line up on the basis of age cohorts or length of time in the order. Those who have been around longer and are older have built up more "side bets" in the order; that is, they have garnered commitments and rewards related to the persistence of the order in its traditional form. Examples of side bets include a sense of identity, assurance of jobs, status in the Church and society, retirement benefits, security, and social networks that are familiar and rewarding. While younger nuns may have options in the job market as well as life-styles outside the order, many older nuns are reluctant to see the traditional system changed because of fewer alternatives open to them. Change, therefore, can be threatening and anxiety provoking. The conflicts that predominate within orders tend to be centered around discussions of change versus maintenance of the status quo rather than around the allocation of scarce resources.

Loss of Morale and the Development of Cynicism among Members

As tension and pressure mount in an organization experiencing declining resources and legitimacy, morale of members tends to sag (Behn, 1978), and high turnover follows (Levine, 1979). The literature on organizational change consistently shows that organizational members become preoccupied with how change will affect them (Greenhalgh, 1983). Simultaneous with the members' eagerness to obtain information regarding possible changes is a common practice among management to withhold information from members as long as possible to avoid the panic and stress such information can arouse. As a result, members in a changing organization tend to feel starved for information and are ripe for the spread of any rumors that may be initiated (Greenhalgh and Jick, 1978; Greenhalgh, 1978).

In the absence of adequate, consistent, and believable information from official sources, members turn to fellow workers to negotiate definitions of the situation (Hirshhorn and Associates, 1983). Informal discussion of organizational decline and its consequences for current members fills the gap left by administrators' reluctance to involve members in adapting and perhaps even dismantling the organizational structure. Rumors, gossip, speculation, and eventual disgruntlement and feeling left out of the process take over, and low morale and alienation result.

Feeling uninformed and having decisions that affect one's life made by those at the top frequently results in the members' developing "cynical knowledge" about what's occurring. Cynical knowledge refers to a realization by members that presumably altruistic actions or procedures of the organization actually maintain the legitimacy of existing authority or preserve the institutional structure (Goldner et al., 1977). Members usually construct among themselves explanations for a variety of organizational circumstances about which they have no direct information but which otherwise make no sense to them. Cynical knowledge is especially prevalent in normative organizations that have a large professional component because in these organizations members expect a higher level of altruistic behavior than in utilitarian, profit-motivated organizations.

In profit-making, bureaucratic organizations most members have no direct responsibility for decisions regarding change or termination. The feelings of those watching things fall apart and seeing little hope for the revitalization of the organization range from emotional disengagement for those who have other options to depression and anger for those who have made high investments in the group and see few alternatives to continuing with the organization until the end. A few with activist leanings may organize to try to prevent dissolution, but, for the most part, members express their feelings in erratic behavior, suspicion and mistrust, self-protective disinterest in the organization, and departure from routine and expected practice (Kanter and Stein, 1979). The "rules" cease to have binding force under conditions of uncertainty. This deviant behavior tends to reinforce a process that promotes further decay because the administration can no longer count on members to continue the ongoing functions of the organization.

People build enormous investments in organizations that go far beyond the stated purpose of the system; these investments—including job security, financial commitments, retirement programs, relationships with people, meaningfulness, a sense of place in society—do not disappear just because the organization is in trouble. As members realize that the organization is experiencing difficult times and that substantial change is imminent, anxiety and stress are usual reactions.

During the 1960s, as the Second Vatican Council was convening in Rome, there was great euphoria and hope within religious orders of women as nuns anticipated and prepared for change. The Sister Formation Movement of the previous decade had readied nuns for change by questioning the adequacy of existing structures in meeting the needs of both members within the orders as well as the people they were serving. This euphoria continued in the late 1960s and well into the next decade as orders began reevaluating their life-style and initiating renewal programs. Most notably, the increased focus upon greater democratization and respect for the individuality and diversity of members created a sense of greater freedom on the part of members.

A major reason articulated by Pope Pius XII in initiating renewal in religious orders was to stem the increasing defections of nuns and to develop a way of life more appealing to modern Catholic girls who might be potential recruits. As renewal proceeded, however, the rates of exodus increased (Ebaugh, 1977; Neal, 1984). By 1965 the number of nuns leaving their orders doubled from the previous year, reaching an all-time high in 1970 when 4,337 nuns left convents in the United States. Simultaneously, the number of recruits declined from its peak in the period from 1963 to 1965, when 32,433 young girls entered religious orders, to a low of 2,590 who entered between 1971 and 1975 (Neal, 1984). While the shrinking membership was of concern to some administrators and nuns in general, the prevailing rationale was that many of those leaving never should have entered in the first place or that they had been challenged to reevaluate their original commitment and now felt they no longer wanted to opt for a celibate, religious life. The overall consensus was that those who remained would have deepened their commitment because leaving no longer had the same stigma in the Catholic community that it had in previous eras.

Only during the 1980s did most orders face the severe personnel and financial issues that resulted from declining membership. The initial realization of these consequences caused some panic and anxiety among nuns. However, in the past several years many orders evidence an interesting phenomenon, reminiscent of Festinger's (1956) theory of cognitive dissonance in which he argues that people tend to reinterpret events in such a way as to irradicate dissonance and make sense of their worlds. It is quite common in orders today to hear nuns accepting the probable demise of institutional religious life as it has been known for centuries and arguing that the "charism" or mission of the orders will continue in a radically new form, perhaps through the "associate" programs that many orders have initiated. Associates are lay people (nonreligious) who want to have a loose affiliation with an order and its mission while still engaged in their family, work, and financial lives independent of the order. Associates join members of the order for prayer, meditation, discussion, liturgy, and organizational meetings; in some instances they also give voluntary service in the settings in which nuns are involved. It is dubious whether these associate programs can exist apart from the continuance of the order, but they provide hope and optimism for nuns in the order who see the perpetuation of their goals in an associate program that is rapidly growing.

As I mentioned earlier, in the past few years it is also becoming more common to hear nuns accept the challenge of "dying gracefully" as an opportunity to witness to the fact that most organizations do not last forever: demise and death are parts of a normal process that must be accepted and experienced with a positive attitude.

Attempts at Environmental Manipulation

Many organizational collapses can be traced to failures of an organization to alter responses in the face of environmental change (Staw et al., 1981). For various reasons, an organization can lose its "environmental niche." A niche is a segment of the larger environment that is bounded by such factors as the availability of resources to support an organization's activities, constraints such as technology and culture, and the presence of consumer demand for organizations' outputs (Cameron and Zammute, 1983).

There is a general tendency for individuals, groups, and organizations to behave rigidly in threatening situations (Staw et al., 1981). When an organization loses an environmental niche—that is, when the products or services of an organization are no longer needed or needed to a lesser extent by the environment—then the organization either (1) retrenches and becomes more rigid and conservative or (2) attempts to redefine a niche in which its resources are valued. If the environmental threat is real, then the first response is usually dysfunctional for the organization in the long run. Although an external threat may lead to greater intragroup solidarity and cohesiveness in the short run (Sherif and Sherif, 1953; Hall and Mansfield, 1971), the long-term effect may be that the group loses its function and purpose in providing resources in the external environment. The Chrysler Corporation, for example, when faced with the oil crisis and rising gasoline prices, continued large production runs on its largest and most fuel-inefficient cars until inventories overflowed. Similarly, the *Saturday Evening Post* continued to raise its prices as circulation dropped (Hall, 1976). In both instances, the companies failed to adapt to the changing environment such that they either collapsed or came close to it.

Successful organizations, however, take steps to redefine an organizational niche under conditions of external threat. When Iacocca took over the Chrysler Corporation, one of his first tasks was to shift the company from big, fuel-inefficient cars to smaller, fuel-efficient vehicles. In Sills's classic study of the March of Dimes, he demonstrates how the Foundation for the Prevention of Infantile Paralysis shifted its goals from the eradication of polio, once the polio vaccine made polio almost nonexistent, to the prevention of birth defects (Sills, 1957).

The establishment of an environmental niche is perhaps the greatest challenge to religious orders today. In the past thirty years many services that orders provided for the Church and society have been replaced by the expansion of private and public bureaucracies. The staffing of parochial schools, for example, has been provided by nuns for the past hundred years. It was common for Catholic immigrant groups to transport nuns from their host country to establish church schools for their children. Many orders historically defined their mission as providing immigrant children an excellent education in a Christian environment.

Many religious orders owned private schools and were able to charge minimal tuition because the schools were staffed by nuns who received minimal salaries. Even in the cases in which schools were owned by parishes, most administrative and teaching positions were held by nuns whom the parish supported by room and board in addition to very small stipends. As certification requirements for educational institutions became more stringent in the United States in the latter half of this century, operation costs increased and placed greater financial burdens on the religious orders and the parishes.

In addition, by the end of the 1960s most religious orders experienced decline in their membership as a result of deaths, defections, and reductions in the number of new recruits to the order. These demographic changes within orders resulted in higher median ages and an increase in the number of elderly and retired nuns no longer able to work. Because of nuns' low salaries for many years and the lack of retirement benefits, orders faced severe financial crises as their membership aged and dependency ratios increased. As a result of financial problems, along with a shift in their perception of their mission, most orders closed their own schools and demanded higher salaries for the nuns who staffed parish-owned schools. Many parishes were unable to pay higher salaries as well as upgrade their schools to meet certification requirements. During the 1970s and 1980s many such schools were closed or consolidated, in attempts to reduce costs.

To support their increasing retirement needs, orders began to place more nuns in lucrative jobs in both public schools and agencies that provided better salaries and benefits. In most orders today, the majority of members are not only working outside the structure of parochial schools but are also no longer in teaching positions. In 1966 58 percent of American nuns were teachers; by 1982 the figure had dropped to 23 percent (Neal, 1984). The nuns who left teaching entered a variety of other jobs; thus, orders that traditionally defined their mission as teaching are necessarily redefining their goals and purpose. Likewise, as governmental regulations and developments in medical technologies changed hospitals into big businesses it was increasingly difficult for religious orders to meet the professional and financial requirements to manage them. Some hospitals traditionally run and staffed by religious orders could not meet the competition of public and for-profit private hospitals and were gradually closed.

As religious orders moved away from their mission to teach, heal, and offer social services in parochial institutions, they were unable to identify a new niche for themselves in either the Church or society. Given the diversity of occupations among members today, it is virtually impossible for religious orders to construct their mission and environmental niche in terms of specific works. Instead, many orders are struggling to redefine their purpose in more abstract, ideological terms such as "the witnessing of Christian values," "standing with the poor of society," and "dedication to furthering the mission of Jesus in the world." But these redefinitions of purpose are more difficult to justify in terms of their necessity in society. As a result, nuns are now hired because of their professional credentials rather than their status as members of religious orders.

Owing to the changes that have occurred in the settings in which nuns have traditionally worked and the fact that occupational diversification has occurred within orders, redefining an environmental niche is a central challenge to orders today. Although orders recognize the necessity for redefinition of purpose, they have not as yet been successful in carving out a niche that is unique and valued by society.

In summary, the major consequences of organizational decline predicted in the literature—centralization of authority, internal allocation of resources, fear of risk taking, intraorganizational turf battles, loss of morale, and environmental manipulation—have not occurred in religious orders as they experience decline. The question now remains: Why are orders not experiencing the consequences that characterize most declining organizations? The following section suggests some possible reasons.

Religious Orders: A Deviant Case of Declining Organizations

For a number of reasons religious orders do not follow the patterns characteristic of other types of declining organizations that have been studied. These reasons fall into two basic categories: (1) structural factors, and (2) ideological stances.

Structural Factors

Religious orders, while relatively independent as organizations, remain a subunit of the Roman Catholic Church. Such attachment to the larger Church does not insulate and protect them from threats of decline, such as financial exigencies, but nuns are very much a part of the theological and liturgical life of the Church as well as required to submit their constitutions to Rome for approval.

Even though fewer nuns are staffing parochial institutions, most nuns are active in the local parishes to which they belong. The changes initiated by Vatican II, in allowing more lay participation in liturgy, folk music in church, democratization of parish and diocesan structures, reinterpretations of doctrine and Scripture, and an attitude of greater openness to the modern world, as well as the growing numbers of Catholics, create an atmosphere of dynamism and excitement that counteracts the retrenchment felt in the orders themselves. Increasingly, nuns are identifying with their local parishes and taking part in activities alongside the lay parishioners.

More and more nuns are being trained as professionals in various jobs, ranging from medical and legal careers to all types of executive positions. Because their jobs no longer depend on assignment by a religious superior, many nuns are gaining confidence in their abilities to perform well as professional women. Unlike the traditional system of religious life, a nun's career can be quite independent of her status as a nun. In fact, it is increasingly common for ex-nuns to keep their jobs even when they sever ties with an order.

In contrast to the previous system of religious life, nuns today are also contributing to social security and, in some cases, to private retirement systems in their work settings. As a result, more and more nuns are secure in professions and the social networks they establish at work, and their diverse living situations. The possibility of organizational demise and even extinction, therefore, is not as threatening as it would have been in the traditional system where every aspect of one's life was tied to the order.

Because most orders accumulated fixed assets, such as land and buildings during their growth periods of the first half of this century, nuns, in many orders, are hopeful that their orders have sufficient resources to sustain their current members throughout their lifetimes. Also, in the past several years, as median ages have risen substantially and retirement needs of older nuns have mushroomed, orders have aggressively engaged in financial planning and are taking the necessary steps to guarantee that members will be cared for. As a result, the panic of financial insecurity that usually accompanies organizational decline is mitigated for members of religious orders.

Finally, and perhaps most important of all the structural factors, the nature of the institution has shifted. Prior to Vatican II, and for most of their history, religious orders have typified the model of total institutions described by Goffman (1961). A total institution is "a place of residence and work where a large number of like-situated individuals, cut off from the wider society for an appreciable period of time, together lead an enclosed, formally administered round of life." The normal barriers separating the sleep, work, and play aspects of life do not exist, and each phase of the members' daily activity is conducted in the company of many others who are treated alike. Decision making is highly centralized and encompasses the whole of the members' lives. Goffman's model of a total institution accurately describes pre–Vatican II orders, but the life-style and structures of contemporary orders more closely resemble a voluntary organization model where only a segment of a person's life is involved and where the organization becomes a resource for the goals of the members (Ebaugh, 1977).

Many aspects of nuns' lives today are independent of their commitment to an order; therefore, organizational decline is less threatening psychologically than it would have been in a more totalistic environment.

From an organizational perspective, the basic challenge for the survival of a voluntary organization is maintaining goals and a sense of purpose to generate the voluntary commitment of members. This is precisely the basic challenge religious orders are facing today.

Ideological Factors

In addition to the structural factors that explain why religious orders are not experiencing the consequences of decline described in the literature, another important explanation for the differences relates to the ideology and meaning system that has developed in religious orders. Pope John XXIII, in his opening address to the Council delegates (1962), set the agenda and established the spirit for renewal. He spoke of the Catholic Church as a pilgrim church that must be open and adaptive to new circumstances that present themselves as the Church moves through this world in search of the heavenly kingdom. By "aggiornamento," his rallying cry for the Council, he referred to the needs of adapting the Church to contemporary conditions and encouraging a mentality of reevaluation and change.

The Council decree on religious life and the implementation documents that followed insisted that every aspect of religious life must come under scrutiny. Those structures that continued to express the essential messages of Scripture and the spirit of an order's founder were to be maintained; those structures and customs that were outdated and hampered the witnessing of the essential messages were to be eradicated or changed to meet the conditions of the modern age.

One consequence of the process of reevaluation and renewal was that nuns came to see their religious orders as human creations rather than sacred institutions. The "institutional awe" in which nuns held the previous system gave way to the realization that structures were humanly created and could therefore be changed by the people in them.

In post–Vatican II theology, the notions of risk taking, challenge, and the courage to question and effect change replaced ideas of sacred tradition and blind obedience to authority. Adaptation and change were presented as Christian challenges in the modern world. The legitimation of critical thinking and the challenge of existing structures laid the psychological groundwork that buffered nuns from many negative consequences that the threat of organizational demise often creates for members, such as a sense of noninvolvement in the change process and the loss of morale that occurs when members feel uninformed of what is happening.

The fact that the renewal process, from its very inception, involved the active participation of nuns also kept them informed and prepared them for the changes that were effected. The fact that very little "cynical knowledge" or secrecy characterizes the decline in religious orders is owing to the systematic attempt to involve every nun in the changes as they occur. Most of the "blame" for the demise of the institution is placed on demographic and social factors rather than on "bad" decisions made by the administration or the members. Decline is seen as inevitable, given the changes in society, the Church, and the orders themselves.

During the renewal process of the last several decades, nuns have focused on maintaining the "mission" or goals of religious orders rather than on maintaining traditional organizational structures. As orders now enter a decline stage, there is hope among nuns that their mission will be continued through other groups in the Church, especially through those lay members who have been trained by nuns and joined the associate programs that are growing in many orders. Although the future of these programs is precarious because they revolve around a central core of nuns, they are providing hope to many nuns who see them as a way of perpetuating commitment to the basic mission and history of the order.

In summary, both structural factors and the ideological changes that have occurred in religious orders in the process of renewal have buffered nuns from many negative consequences that usually accompany organizational decline and death.

 **CHAPTER 4**

Demographic Changes
of American Nuns

The challenges currently being faced by religious orders of women in the United States are owing, in large part, to the demographic shifts that have occurred in their membership during the past twenty-five years. Not only has the population in religious orders declined, but the membership characteristics of those who remain differ significantly from previous decades. To understand the organizational changes that have occurred, it is important to begin with an analysis of demographic shifts in membership.

In *Out of the Cloister: A Study of Organizational Dilemmas* (1977) I focus on the influences that lead to demographic changes in religious orders. In this book, my focus is primarily upon the impact of demographic shifts on the structure and viability of orders. The purpose of this chapter is threefold: (1) to describe membership statistics in religious orders in the United States during the past twenty-five years in order to demonstrate that religious orders signify a declining institution; (2) to introduce the order I have selected for intensive case study and to demonstrate that it is, in fact, representative of religious orders in this country; and (3) to trace the origins of the case study order in Europe and its early history in the United States.

Demographic Characteristics of U.S. Religious Orders of Women

In 1950 there were 147,310 Catholic women in religious orders in the United States. That number grew each year throughout the 1950s and early 1960s and reached its apex in 1965, the year that marked the closing of the Second Vatican Council. The Official Catholic Directory reports a total membership of 179,954 for that year. In the years

FIGURE 4.1

Number of Women in Catholic Religious Orders in the U.S. by Year

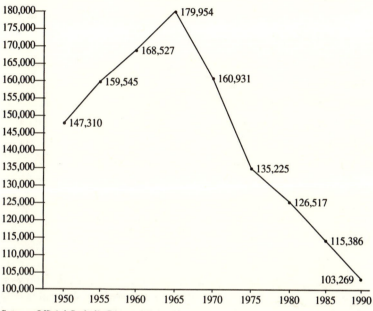

Source: *Official Catholic Directory.*

following the Council, however, the trend began to reverse itself. By 1970 the number of religious women in the U.S. dropped to 160,931, an 10% decrease over five years. The official statistic for number of religious women in 1975 was 135,225; by 1980 the number had declined further to 126,517, and by 1990 to 103,269. Between 1965 and 1990, therefore, 76,685 fewer religious nuns existed in the United States, a 43 percent decrease.

The decline in membership in religious orders of women over the past twenty-five years is explained by a decrease in rates of entry and an increase in defections of members, along with mortality rates for those in religious orders. The most comprehensive demographic data available on rates of entry and defection within religious orders was collected as part of the National Sisters' Survey sponsored by the Conference of Major Superiors of Women (CMSW) and carried out by Marie Augusta Neal, S.N.D. The first survey was conducted in 1966 with 88 percent (437) of religious orders responding to a comprehen-

TABLE 4.1
Entering Trends 1950 through 1980

	# New Recruits	# Women Making Final Vows	Recruits Making Final Vows (in percentages)
1948–1952	23,302	16,320	70
1953–1957	27,157	18,168	67
1958–1962	32,433	No data	No data
1963–1965	18,316	No data	No data
1966–1970	8,699	4,408	51
1971–1975	2,590	1,986	77
1976–1980	2,767	No data	No data

Source: Modified from Neal, 1984: 20.

sive organizational survey (Neal 1970, 1971). In 1982 a follow-up survey was conducted; it replicated and extended the original survey (Neal 1981, 1984). Data from these two surveys provide a longitudinal analysis of what occurred in religious orders over the sixteen-year period, from 1966–1982, immediately following the Second Vatican Council. The following statistics on rates of entry and exit are based on data from the two surveys.

Declining Rates of Entry

In the 1966 survey, orders were asked how many new recruits entered at various time periods between 1950 and 1966. As indicated in Table 4.1, between 1948 and 1952, 23,302 young Catholic women entered religious orders. That number continued to increase each year of the 1950s and for the first two years of the 1960s. From 1958 to 1962, 32,433 young women entered religious orders in the United States. Between 1963 and 1965, the years of the Council, the trend began to reverse itself. In the five-year period between 1966 and 1970 only 8,699 recruits entered, 73 percent fewer than in the five-year period

TABLE 4.2
Leaving Trends from 1950 through 1980

	# Leaving	Before Final Vows	After Final Vows
1950	381	no data	no data
1955	590	no data	no data
1960	765	no data	no data
1965	1,562	no data	no data
1970	4,337	1,723	2,614
1975	1,191	294	897
1980	751	147	604

Source: Neal, 1984: 21.

between 1958 and 1962. From 1976 to 1980 only 2,767 recruits entered, 91 percent fewer than in the 1958–1962 period.

In addition to calculating the number entering each year, it is important to determine how many remain because exodus rates are high during the first few years after entrance. Because canon law of the Catholic Church requires a recruit to go through a number of progressive stages of socialization (affiliate, candidate, novice), one way to ascertain retention is to determine number at each stage for various time periods. Comparing these statistics for 1966 and 1982, the following pattern is evident: in 1966 there were 4,376 affiliates, or first-stage recruits, compared with 642 in 1982; in 1966 there were 3,406 candidates, or second-stage recruits, compared with 569 in 1982; and in terms of novices, the final stage before taking religious vows, there were 7,257 in 1966 and 780 in 1982. One fact is clearly evident: entrance rates into religious orders decreased dramatically in the fifteen years following the Council.

Increased Rates of Defection

Simultaneous with decreased rates of women entering religious orders during the 1960s and 1970s was an increased rate of defection on the part of members within the orders. Although a small number of religious left each year prior to the mid 1960s, by 1965 the trickle became a flood that was difficult to contain (see Table 4. 2).

In 1950, 381 women left religious orders in the United States; by 1965 this number rose to 1,562 and rose again to 2,015 in 1966. The trend of high defection rate continued to rise in the latter 1960s and reached its high point in 1970 when 4,337 religious women left their convents and returned to secular life. During the decade of the 1970s the tide of defections slowed down, in part because those who wanted to leave had done so by that point (Ebaugh, 1977). The 1980 defection figure of 751 resembles the 765 figure of those who left twenty years earlier. The storm of membership loss seemed to be subsiding. However, the membership demographics of religious orders after the storm—considering both decreased rates of recruitment and increased rates of defection—reflects in a very different population that has had far-reaching organizational consequences.

Membership Characteristics

The most dramatic outcome of the lowered entrance rate and increased defection rate for religious orders was their impact upon the age structure of those who remained in the orders. Just as the birthrate (along with the death rate) in a population is a primary determinant of the median age of the population, within organizations that depend on young recruits for replenishment the number of those entering influences the overall median age of the members. During the years in which religious orders were recruiting large numbers of young women, median ages were quite low. However, as soon as entrance rates began to slow down, median ages of the membership began to rise.

In 1966 17 percent of U.S. religious women were over age sixty-five. By 1982 that percentage rose to 38 percent, a 30.9 percent increase (Neal, 1984). The fact that median age in religious orders has risen so rapidly in the past several decades is the major reason that orders are not only facing severe organizational problems today but also anticipating that they may not survive the current crisis. Just as populations with little or no natural increase have died off in the course of history, so too have organizations and groups that are not replenishing themselves with new members faded away over time.

Stagnant population growth and high median age have implications and reverberations throughout the system: financial, occupational, health related, effect upon authority structures, mechanisms of socialization, and articulation with the external environment. In the following chapters I trace these implications in terms of the case study order.

The Sisters of Service

Prior to the Second Vatican Council (1962–1965), religious orders of women in the Catholic Church were homogeneous in both purpose and structural characteristics. Their histories varied, and the particular religious flavor imparted by their founders differed somewhat; but in general Catholic convents constituted a unique form of social organization that was easily characterized. Goffman's (1961) description of convents as a type of "total institution" aptly captured the organization of pre–Vatican II orders. Likewise, the Religious Community Survey (1966), sent to the superior general of most orders in the United States, revealed the similarity of organizational structure and life-style that existed among religious orders in the year following the close of the Council.

That homogeneity among orders, however, soon dissipated as they began implementing the Council's mandate to experiment with new forms of organization more appropriate to conditions of the modern world. In the decade between 1966 and 1976, every order was asked to reevaluate its constitution in the light of a return to the sources of all Christian life and an adjustment of the community to the changed conditions of the times ("Decree on the Appropriate Renewal of Religious Orders," 1965). Furthermore, each order was mandated to prepare a blueprint of its program for experimentation and ultimately to submit a new constitution to Rome based on those two principles. During the decade of experimentation, orders varied in both the pace and nature of their response to the Council's call for renewal and adaptation. As a result, the homogeneity in structure and life-style gave way to greater divergence among orders.

In my 1970 study of convents (Ebaugh, 1977), degree of structural change was a major variable in predicting rates of defection. On the basis of a national organizational survey of religious orders, I found sufficient variation among orders to be able to show relationships between degree of change and such outcomes as recruitment and defection patterns. Because of the organizational differences among orders, I was able to construct an organizational change index that allowed me to select one order that represented a change-oriented order, one that reflected a nonchange-oriented order, and a third order that represented moderate change orders.

By the decade of the 1980s most orders had completed their experimentation period and institutionalized structural change. Because religious orders as part of a highly centralized Catholic Church experienced the same opportunities and constraints in the change process, the outcome was that the renewed orders were again homogeneous in structure and ideology. By 1982 when the national Sisters' Survey was replicated (Neal, 1984), the data indicate relatively little variation among orders in major demographics (e.g., median age, rates of recruitment and defection, educational attainment of members) and organizational structures such as government, finances, dress, apostolic works, and life-style of members. For example, in 1966 (in the first Sisters' Survey) 79 percent of the orders accepted recruits with only a high school diploma; by 1982, only 12 percent accepted recruits with only a high school education. Most orders (63 percent) required some work experience, and 42 percent also required some college. Likewise, in 1966 only 3.6 percent of the orders had introduced personal and local community budgets; by 1982 89 percent of all orders insisted on personal budgets. In 1966 28 percent of the orders involved the membership in decision making; by 1988 this figure had risen to 84 percent. By 1982 it was obvious that religious orders of women had undergone dramatic changes and, in many ways, bore little resemblance to their pre–Vatican II forms. Also obvious, however, is that orders were again demographically and structurally homogeneous and facing similar problems and challenges in terms of organizational survival.

In writing this book, my initial intention was to follow the three orders I had studied in 1970 to see what changes they effected in the intervening twenty years. As I began investigating the three cases, however, I realized that the differences among the orders, evident in 1970, had virtually disappeared and that the orders had evolved very similar structures; today there were more similarities than differences among them. Because one goal for the current study is to provide an in-depth description of religious orders as they appear in 1990, I decided that, given the homogeneity among orders, I could provide a richer analysis by focusing upon one case study rather than trying to decipher minor differences between orders. Such differences might be meaningful to those who are members of religious orders or Church folk who are very knowledgeable about religious life, but they mean little to sociologists interested in religious life as an institution. I decided, therefore, to select one order that was representative of religious orders in the United States and to conduct an intensive case analysis of this order.

I selected the Sisters of Service (a pseudonym) for two reasons. First, on the basis of both the 1966 Community Survey (Neal, 1984) and the 1982 follow-up survey, the Sisters of Service community was typical of orders throughout the United States in the circumstances of its founding, its history in the United States, its demographic profiles, its involvement in the Sister Formation Movement and the educational development of its members, the pace and substance of the changes created in the order in the decades following Vatican II, and, finally, the challenges facing the order as a result of these changes.

Second, because of the location of the motherhouse of the order as well as the living situations of many members, I was able to take part in many activities of the order, be present at various types of functions, interview members at all levels of the organization, and maintain an ongoing dialogue with members of the order over a two-year period.

Methodology

I obtained data regarding the Sisters of Service from a variety of sources, including participant observation, interviews, and historical documents. From April 1989 through July 1990 I attended two general assemblies in the order; each meeting lasted about three days. I was invited not only to attend the formal sessions but also to live at the motherhouse campus during the assemblies. These living arrangements allowed me to be part of the informal discussions that took place in the dining rooms and hallways where the nuns socialized between sessions.

During the fifteen months of fieldwork I conducted formal interviews with twenty-five members in the order. Given the fact that I was interested in organizational data rather than individual opinions or attitudes, I selected interviewees on the basis of their position in the organization. In addition to the superior general and each member of the general council, I interviewed those individuals in charge of specific offices such as formation, finances, and ministry work. Because I was interested in structural changes that have occurred in religious orders in the past several decades, as well as projections regarding the future of orders, I disproportionately selected younger members who are involved in "new ministries" as well as nontraditional living arrangements.

I conducted intensive interviews with two retired nuns, over the age of seventy, ten people between the ages of forty and sixty-five, three nuns with final vows in their thirties, and three members who had not yet made their permanent commitment in the group. Beyond individual opinions and attitudes, I asked each interviewee how others in her age cohort were responding to events and issues in the order.

In addition to participant observation and interviews, I was provided with historical documents, administrative reports, official constitutions and by-laws, and reports from various committees. Much historical information on the order came from several books published by members. To preserve the anonymity of the order, I have omitted direct reference to these works.

After completing the final manuscript I asked four members of the order to read it to assure anonymity, accuracy, and the respect that I sincerely feel for this group of women.

History of the Sisters of Service

The Sisters of Service was founded in 1762 by a Roman Catholic priest in France. As he traveled to rural parishes throughout France as an itinerant preacher, he noted that the children were not being educated, even in the basic skills of reading and writing. He formulated a plan to train local girls to be teachers for these children; he sought girls who could lead the life of the poorest of the villagers, who were so zealous for God's poor that they would abandon all material possessions to dedicate their lives in the service of education and who were strong enough to endure poverty, mistreatment, and even persecution. He found these qualities in one woman, a factory worker in a rural village who was coming to him for spiritual counseling. During an illness, she had taught herself to read and was organizing factory girls to learn to read during their lunch hours. The priest invited her to come under his tutelage to be trained further in both educational skills and spiritual development.

In time, several other village girls asked to join the young woman in her good works. Simultaneously, a wealthy woman heard about the priest's efforts and offered her home and assistance in preparing these girls to teach. When the priest felt his teachers were sufficiently prepared, he applied for and received permission to open schools in nearby villages.

Initially, the group of women teachers were loosely organized. Even though they lived together whenever possible and continued to be counseled by the priest, they had no formalized structure and were not recognized by the Catholic Church as a religious order.

As is typical of institutions, growth and prosperity created the necessity of organization and standard practices that would accommodate larger numbers, unify members, and give them identity as a group. As a result, by 1839 the Sisters of Service were using a constitution to guide their lives, wearing a distinctive habit, professing the three simple vows of poverty, chastity, and obedience, and associating with five or six different motherhouses, all loosely connected with each other.

In 1852 a bishop from America arrived at the motherhouse of the Sisters of Service to solicit sisters to go with him to minister to the immigrants who had settled in the United States. The adventure of ministering to immigrants who were struggling to survive in a foreign land appealed to two of the sisters who agreed to accompany him. This marked the beginning of the order in the United States.

For the first sixteen years, the Sisters of Service group was headquartered in a southern town in the United States, where the members taught in parish schools. In the hopes of recruiting more local girls into the order and ministering to immigrants from the region where the motherhouse of the order was located, in 1868 the order relocated its headquarters from a southern city to a rural settlement where almost all the inhabitants were Catholic and in dire need of someone to teach their children.

A major goal of the fledgling order was to attract more young girls to enter the group so that more schools could be opened in surrounding areas. A number of girls entered between 1868 and 1878, but most did not stay. To root the order in this country and assure its survival, it was necessary for one sister to return to the motherhouse in France in 1878 to solicit more European sisters to join those in the United States. Eight women came back to America to join the efforts of the few sisters already working there. This pattern of recruitment of sisters from Europe continued into the early decades of the twentieth century. Over the years, sister recruiters traveled to not only France and Germany for additional sisters but also Ireland and Poland, very Catholic countries that had large numbers in their convents. During a recruiting trip made in 1883, for example, fifty-two European sisters volunteered to work as Sisters of Service in the U.S. province.

With these sisters as a solid foundation, the number of local recruits began to increase. With size came the necessity of erecting permanent buildings to house the sisters and greater independence from the motherhouse in France in order to make the administrative decisions that faced the sisters on a daily basis. In 1892 the Sisters of Service in the United States became an independent diocesan order under the jurisdiction of the local bishop with their own constitution and administrator, known as a superior general. The order remained under diocesan control until 1912 when it received approbation as a pontifical order; that is, its constitution was approved by Rome, and the order came under the direct jurisdiction of the Vatican.

When it was decided in 1896 that the Southern Pacific Railroad would not be built through the community in which the order was headquartered, but rather in a nearby town, the order realized that the local community would never be a hub of activity and growth. It was a custom in the order that every sister, regardless of where she was teaching, came to the motherhouse for the summer months in order to continue her educational training, attend the annual spiritual retreat, and associate with other members of the congregation; this necessitated train travel because the stagecoach was limited in its routes and capacity. To have access to a major railroad it was therefore decided to relocate to the neighboring town. In 1896, both the new motherhouse and an academic academy for girls were opened there.

In 1903, 250 Sisters of Service taught in fifty-five schools. This was an increase of 155 members in the years since the congregation became independent. Given the ever increasing state demands for educational credentials for certified teachers, it became necessary to offer more and more advanced courses for the sisters who came home in the summertime for continued education. In fact, there were pressures by the state to have certified teachers with college degrees teaching in state-approved schools. As a result, more and more college-level courses were introduced in the academy associated with the motherhouse. During the summer the sisters attended these classes, and during the school year, the academy served as a boarding school for both high school and college students.

With the progressive education movement in the United States during the 1920s and 1930s came increased emphasis on not only grammar school education for all children but also high school training. To meet this need, by 1925 the Sisters of Service had opened twenty-five high schools in the United States. In addition, in 1925 the general chapter (the governing body of the order) expanded the goals of the order to include care of sick, especially in hospital settings. Health care had become a pressing need with the expanding U.S. population. The Sisters of Service responded to this need by allowing sisters interested in the health field to obtain nursing degrees.

By the decades of the 1950s and 1960s, the Sisters of Service formed a well-established congregation in the United States with an impressive campus that housed not only a motherhouse for the order but also a retirement center for the sisters, a Gothic chapel that was recognized as one of the most beautiful in the Southwest, a high school that attracted Catholic girls from not only the United States but also Latin America and Central America, and an accredited college housed in numerous buildings on a 115-acre campus. The order owned and/or staffed educational institutions in three states as well as a catechetical center in Mexico, run by native Mexican nuns affiliated with the order.

The order was experiencing the numerical growth characteristic of most orders in the United States at that time, owing to the large influx of Catholic girls who entered religious orders in the middle decades of this century. At the time that Pope John XXIII announced that he was convening an ecumenical council to reevaluate and update the Catholic Church, the Sisters of Service, like most orders in the United States, was at a high point in its growth, in terms of numbers of members as well as the financial stability of the order. In the twenty-five years

TABLE 4.3
Number of Vowed Members in the Sisters of Service, 1950–1990

Year	# Members	% Change
1950	703	—
1955	732	+ 0.04
1960	727	– 0.007
1965	730	+ 0.004
1970	687	– 0.06
1975	600	– 0.12
1980	547	– 0.09
1985	491	– 0.10
1990	432	– 0.12

Note: Figures derived from in-house data of the order's membership records.

after Vatican II the demographics of the order changed dramatically, reflecting what was happening nationwide to religious orders and causing the order to face the consequences of organizational decline.

Membership Demographics

The Sisters of Service was originally established as a teaching order. Even though the goals of the order are more diverse today, 33 percent of the members are still employed in the educational sector. Like most orders in the United States, occupational diversity of members entails all kinds of jobs, including social services, adult education, special education, migrant education, midwifery, legal aid, foreign service positions, and community organizing.

In 1965 the order numbered 730 members; by 1990 that number had declined to 432. Like the national trend, the decrease was owing to fewer recruits and a greater rate of defection. In 1966, seventeen candidates sought admission into the order; also seventeen novices had been accepted into the order that year. By 1982, those numbers declined to three candidates and one novice. In 1990, one candidate sought admission and one novice had been accepted.

Table 4.3 depicts membership trends in the order between 1950 and 1990. As the table indicates, the population of the order declined by 104 permanent members in the fourteen-year period immediately after Vatican II. More important, however, is the fact that the decline is owing to the loss of members in the younger cohorts, that is, among those entering the order and those who opt to remain as permanently vowed members. The selective loss resulted in a skewed age distribution, with median age of members rising significantly each year.

In addition to fewer new recruits, the order lost 116 members between 1966 and 1981. The majority of those who left were younger sisters, in their twenties, who opted not to renew their temporary vows. Although a steady stream left between 1960 and 1975, the order lost the largest number of people in 1970 when nine temporary professed members decided not to renew vows and ten members with final vows requested a dispensation from their commitments.

The fact that those leaving were predominantly young members, coupled with the severe decline in recruitment resulted in a dramatic increase in median age of members. In 1990, the median age of members reached seventy, which means that 50 percent of the members were aged seventy or older. This fact has profound implications for the order, both financially and organizationally. The remaining chapters of this book are devoted to an analysis of the impact of membership decline and high median age upon various structures in the order, including authority, finances, recruitment and formation of members, goals and mission, life-styles of members, maintaining a sense of community, and the commitment of the order to feminist issues.

CHAPTER 5

Authority

Although the changes in religious orders during the past twenty-five years have affected every aspect of their structure, the accompanying evolution in the authority structure is the most significant. Not only has the system of government changed, but the meaning and rationale of obedience and commitment to the institution have also shifted. Unlike what the literature on declining organizations would predict, the Sisters of Service, under conditions of decline, moved dramatically from a centralized, highly authoritarian system to one of greater democracy and decentralization.

In this chapter I contrast the authority structure as it existed in the Sisters of Service community in 1965 with that of 1990. In addition, I describe the transition period in terms of shifts in theology that prompted structural changes as well as the types of experimental structures that predated the current system.

What has happened in religious orders in recent decades cannot be understood without understanding the fundamental theological changes that underlie the organizational changes. Not only did religious orders set out to experiment with new ways of doing things and relating to each other as members of the group, but, more important, meaning systems and rationales for action were reevaluated and restructured.

Meaning systems are part of the core culture of every group. Group norms, values, interests, behaviors, and customs make no sense to an outsider until these meaning systems are understood because they define the whys and wherefores of group life. These meaning systems are incorporated into a comprehensive thought system, or interpretation of the world, that makes sense to group members and is accepted as the ultimate explanation of reality. Sorel (1941) defines such a comprehensive thought system as a myth, that is, a world view that attempts to explain why certain phenomena were, are, or shall be. The term myth, as sociologists use it, has nothing to do with its popular use to mean mythical, fantasy, or unreal. Rather, the relative truth or untruth of a myth is unimportant. Members do not *understand* a myth; instead, they feel, experience, and believe in it as the ultimate explanation for what is. Members are less interested in proving the myth than in living it out in daily life. Consensual validation by the group sustains the myth—the fact that others also believe it and are willing to live out their lives in terms of it.

Arbuckle (1988) describes a myth as a story of tradition that claims to enshrine a fundamental truth or inner meaning about the world and human life. Myths are deeply serious insights about reality without which people are unable to determine what things really are, what to do with them, or how to relate to them. Arbuckle argues that change and revitalization in any group occurs when fundamental myths shift and are reconceptualized.

Myths, as Joseph Campbell (1968, 1988) points out, provide meaning in response to four basic human needs: (1) a satisfying reason for existence; (2) a coherent cosmology, that is, to know where we fit within a comprehensive world; (3) social organization, along with supportive attitudes, so that we can work together in some kind of harmony, and (4) an inspirational vision that inculcates within us a sense of pride in belonging to a group.

Authority in Pre–Vatican II Religious Orders

The myth that motivated and sustained pre–Vatican II religious orders was the basic myth of Christianity. Religious orders viewed their purpose as total dedication to living a Christian life and thereby giving example to others of a perfect way of life. Members did this by going into a cloister in order to concentrate solely upon living the life Jesus preached for all Christians.

Christian redemption, as seen by the nun, was not an act completed two thousand years ago on a hill in Galilee but was rather a continuous process accomplished by the death of the individual to all worldly attitudes, motivations, and actions and rebirth to a life imbued with supernatural, otherworldly motivations. The two-pronged process of death to oneself and rebirth to God summarized the meaning behind all the highly routinized and institutionalized modes of behavior characteristic of the fifteen centuries of religious orders.

The Meaning of Authority

Central to the Christian myth was the notion that God made His will known through duly appointed superiors, including the pope, cardinals, bishops, priests, and, within religious orders, superiors. Superiors were viewed as more than human authority figures; like the hierarchy in the larger Church, they were viewed as instruments of God whereby the divine will was made known to people. Disobedience, therefore, was more than simple human disobedience warranting punishment. It was an act of pride against God and a rejection of His divine will.

The Sisters of Service, like all women in Catholic orders, professed a vow of obedience whereby they committed themselves to faithfully obeying their superiors. The vow of obedience was formally restricted to specific mandates of superiors, but the spirit of the vow was generalized to the most minute aspects of daily life. For example, each local house of nuns was required to submit an horarium, daily schedule of events, to the superior general who either approved or disapproved it as the will of God for those nuns. Nuns were required to ask permission to stay up later than approved, go to the doctor, use the telephone, visit their families, or take personal articles such as toothpaste or soap from the common closet. While their formal vow of obedience did not explicitly extend to such inconsequential actions, the spirit of the vow was that the superior had the God-given right to determine whether such actions were in accord with God's purposes.

To enable superiors to act as God's representatives, the myth of religious life held that superiors were endowed with the "grace of office," a special gift that enabled superiors to make wise decisions. Superiors, therefore, were endowed with institutional charisma, a special quality associated with not their individual performances or character, but their offices. It was irrelevant, therefore, whether nuns liked or respected their superiors as persons; what was important was the superiors' authority exercised by virtue of their office.

Formal Structure of Authority

The myth of obedience to superiors and thereby obedience to God was operationalized in the official authority structure of the order. In the Sisters of Service, as in most religious orders prior to Vatican II, the highest governing body was the general chapter, a group of representatives elected by the members. The chapter met in secret enclave every six years to elect a central administration, including the superior general and her council, and to formulate general policies. The secrecy that characterized the chapter meetings created a sense of mystique and awe regarding the proceedings and policies of the chapter and encapsulated the outcomes with an aura of legitimacy and extraordinary power. The members of the order knew little or nothing regarding how decisions were made. They were simply announced as official policy and framed in the context of the vow of obedience.

Because few changes were made in the constitution of the order for many years, the primary task of the chapter was to elect the superior general, who then exercised considerable power in the administration of the order. She had the power to assign jobs to members, to decide where and with whom they were to live, what daily schedule they were to follow, and who the local superior was in each house where the members resided.

The superior general, according to the constitution of the order, was the executive officer of the corporation with the responsibility to deal with external groups. Her task was also to govern and administer the internal life of the order. She was given the right, after consultation with her council, to select local superiors, administrators of congregationally owned institutions, and directors of internal ministries such as recruitment and socialization of new members. She had the right to accept or reject candidates for vowed membership in the order. In addition, it was her responsibility to make sure that members were faithful to their vows and to the commitment they made to live religious lives. She exercised social control against not only major infractions on the part of members but also minor ones.

Local superiors, appointed by the superior general to administer local houses of nuns, were bound to ensure that members observed the constitution as well as the customs of the order. Because of their appointment, they shared in the "grace of office" and were viewed as vehicles of the voice of God for the individual nun. Not only did they have the right to assign duties and responsibilities in the local house and to establish the daily schedules for those in their charge, but they were also given the responsibility to assure that nuns in the local house were living exemplary religious lives.

The nuns were instructed by the constitution to obey their superiors and be submissive to them in both small and large matters. At the superior's voice, all were instructed to be ready to obey instantly and willingly. Because it was impossible for the superior herself to see and hear all things, the nuns were commanded to manifest to the superior all personal errors, defects, and temptations and to be willing to be corrected and accept punishment. Once a month the local superior presided over the "chapter of faults," a time of confession when each nun was obligated to publicly confess transgressions against the constitution and rules of the order. The superior forgave the transgressions and administered appropriate punishment.

To acknowledge and reinforce the sacred position held by superiors in the order, the constitution carefully described an "order of precedence," by which the superior general held first place followed by her councillors, the secretary general, and treasurer general. Next came local superiors and then the nuns according to the time of their profession of vows, from the oldest to the youngest members. Normally, nuns had places in chapel, the dining room, and study areas according to their rank.

Because they represented the voice of God in the order, superiors were considered sacred and rituals of respect were developed around them. For example, nuns rose when a superior entered a room and allowed her to proceed through doorways. It was disrespectful to walk in front of a superior unless she gave permission to do so. Nuns attended to her personal needs such as making her bed, cleaning her room, and keeping her clothes laundered and mended. All these rituals reinforced a sense of awe and respect for superiors and their authority, not by virtue of personal qualities, but the charisma associated with their office.

Acceptance of the rigid, hierarchical system of authority was rooted in the generalized myth that permeated every aspect of life in the order, a meaning system that interpreted authority as a direct line from God. The consensual validation whereby all members accepted and respected the interpretation meant not only that the system went unchallenged but also that the nuns valued a system whereby they were privileged to know God's will in their lives.

Consequences of the System

The system of authority as it existed within the order in 1965 had far-reaching effects upon both the institution and its members. Institutionally, the system was organized to effect absolute control over the members. The facts that the legitimating myth was grounded in sacred meanings and defined authority as an avenue of the divine will's expression gave the authority system the quality of what Lifton (1961) calls "mystical manipulation." By that he referred to a mechanism of thought control that involves the creation of a sense of higher purpose, of having inside knowledge of a higher goal. Any thought or purpose that questions the higher one is considered backward, selfish, and petty in the face of the divine ordinance. The person is asked to accept the higher purpose on the basis of absolute trust "like a child in the arms of his mother," a mother who takes care of everything. By defining authority as supernatural, members were obeying not only natural authority but also the divine will of God himself who would certainly take care of those who trusted in him. To disobey was considered sinful and deserving of divine punishment. This mystical sense of obedience extended to the most minute details of members' lives, such as times of rising and retiring, times to pray, eat, speak, keep silent, and recreate.

To the members who vowed to obey superiors, the system of authority and the myth in which it was embedded provided assurance that the superiors knew God's designs for them, in not only major aspects of life but also the daily tasks of living. This assurance created a sense of purpose and security. As long as nuns obeyed their superiors, they could rest assured that they were in God's good standing. Questioning the wisdom of decisions or soul-searching scrutiny of what was expected of oneself in life was unnecessary, a transgression against one's vow of obedience.

The authority system in religious orders prior to Vatican II was embedded in and mirrored the theology and structure of the larger Catholic Church. Religious orders were a microcosm of the authority structure in the hierarchical Church, with the pope as the infallible supreme ruler who was the primary arbiter of truth and holiness. The cardinals and bishops served as subordinate officers carrying out the orders of the pope, with parish priests implementing decisions made above them. Canon law buttressed this system by specifying that obedience to the hierarchy was a requirement of being a Catholic in "good standing" with the Church. In addition, a sense of "institutional awe" and respect for the clergy functioned as one of the many control mechanisms that the Church used to assure that members remained obedient and subservient to the hierarchy.

The notion of papal infallibility, which theologically applies only to certain doctrinal pronouncements of the pope, carried for the laity the generalized notion that the pope had the God-given authority to speak the truth in all matters, spiritual and temporal. The aura of authority filtered down through the hierarchical ranks such that bishops and local priests were also considered dispensers of truth even in the most minute matters of faith and morals.

Catholic girls who entered religious orders were well socialized into this hierarchical authority structure in the Church and were, therefore, primed to generalize the notion of authority to religious superiors in the order. Both explicitly and implicitly superiors were viewed as sharing in the God-given hierarchical authority exercised in the Church.

Transition Years

In the several decades prior to the Second Vatican Council (1962–1965) pressure mounted within the ranks of the Church to redefine the traditional image of authority and to allow greater collegiality and power on the part of clergy and laity. Greater democracy in Western countries and the rumblings toward greater democracy in the third world countries caused many people to begin to question the rigid, authoritarian structures that still prevailed in the Church. In addition, movements like the worker-priest in Europe and the growing Catholic Action around the world gave priests and laity the experience of greater participation in Church affairs. Other Catholics wanted changes in the laws and regulations affecting marriage and education, the Mass, the sacraments, the inquisitorial and condemnatory procedures of the Holy Office, and a redefinition of the rights and duties of bishops, priests, and laymen in the Church's structure (Rynne, 1968).

As the cardinals and bishops gathered in Rome for the first session of the Council, many of the above concerns entered their debates. Cardinal Suenens of Brussels is credited with challenging the conservatives at the Council who favored retaining the traditional hierarchical image of the Church and suggesting that a totally new image be substituted, one that visualized the Church as the People of God, working together to accomplish God's kingdom on earth (Rynne, 1968). In the meeting hall, his proposal met with loud applause, indicating widespread agreement with his proposal.

The progressives at the Council won a major victory in their insistence that the hierarchical image of the Church be replaced by one that visualized the Church as a chosen people who together struggle to know God's will for humankind and work to effect His kingdom on earth. The final document on the Church devotes an entire chapter to the description of the Church as the "new people of God"; it emphasizes the human and communal side of the Church rather than the institutional and hierarchical aspects that characterized previous conceptualizations (Ebaugh, 1991). Among those who have analyzed the council documents most agree that the image of the Church as the "People of God" is the dominant ecclesial image throughout the Council documents (Dulles, 1988). While retaining the doctrine of papal infallibility in regard to major doctrinal pronouncements, the Council put the papacy into a significantly new context. The college of bishops, together with the pope as its head, was seen as having the fullness of power in the Church. The individual bishops were seen not as mere lieutenants of the pope but as pastors in their own right.

The Council articulated two major principles to guide the practice of authority in the post–Council Church: collegiality and subsidiarity. Collegiality was defined as the sharing of power at all levels in the Church. Just as the pope is surrounded by a college of bishops, so each bishop serves as head of a presbyterial college and governs his diocese in consultation with the priests, religious, and laity in his diocese. Pastors, according to the constitution on the Church, "understand that it is their noble duty so to shepherd the faithful and recognize their services and charismatic gifts that all according to their proper roles may cooperate in this common undertaking with one heart."

The principle of subsidiarity signifies that higher levels of authority must respect the capacities, competencies, and tasks of individuals and communities so that a healthy and vigorous life, adapted to different situations, can develop. In practical terms, subsidiarity implies that decisions are made at the level at which they will be implemented in order to call upon the competencies of those involved in the action.

The themes of Church as People of God and the guiding principles of collegiality and subsidiarity run through all the Council documents and provide the rationale for the structural changes implemented after the Council. These structural changes were both numerous and consequential in terms of the daily life of the Church. They included the establishment of a synod of bishops as advisory to the pope, priests' senates in every diocese to advise the bishop, parish councils to make policy decisions on the local parish level, tribunals and lay groups of all kinds to provide input and share in the tasks of local bishops and priests. After centuries of a hierarchical structure, the Church was returning to the model of the early Christian communities that were organized more democratically and collegially.

The shift in conceptualization of authority was evident throughout the council document on "The Appropriate Renewal of Religious Life," the decree that mandated religious orders reevaluate every aspect of their life-styles in order to bring them in accord with the gospel and original inspiration of their founder or foundress and in tune with contemporary historical circumstances. The implementation decree (*Ecclesiae Sanctae*), which was issued a year later, reinforced the principles of collegiality and subsidiarity that characterized the process of renewal as well as the outcome of renewal and adaptation. Specifically, the evaluation process was designed to provide for the input and involvement of every nun in the order.

Permeating the Council decree to religious orders is the notion of Church as a pilgrim people with clerics and laity mutually involved in the journey. Traditionally, men and women in religious orders in the Church were accorded special status, somewhere between cleric and laity. The new document makes it clear that religious are laity by virtue of their baptism and confirmation. Their religious vows do not promote them to a higher status; they merely confer on the religious the responsibility to live the lay state to its perfection.

In response to the Council decree on religious life and its mandate for renewal and adaptation within religious orders, the Sisters of Service immediately began preparing for their renewal chapter scheduled for the summers of 1967 and 1968. Unlike previous chapters, the membership was highly involved in preparing for this chapter, in both electing delegates and forging the agenda. The sisters were encouraged to participate in discussion groups established to reconsider every aspect of religious life as it was being lived in the order, including government, the vows, the purpose and mission of the order, finances, education of the sisters, recruitment and formation of members, and the daily life-style of the members. The committees met for several months prior to the renewal chapter and generated position papers to be debated by the chapter delegates as part of their policy-making function.

Among the major changes instituted after the renewal chapter were the development of a regional system of governance and the establishment of the first local community without a local superior. One of the first efforts to decentralize government and encourage greater collegiality was the system of regional administration in which regional superiors were assigned to members in different geographical regions. Three such regions were delineated. The "regional superiors," as they were called, had no actual authority except to give permissions for minor actions. They supplied informational liaison between the superior general and the individual sister. They were given the tasks of explaining policy decisions to the members and, in turn, listening to the needs and concerns of members and relaying them to higher administration. They also had input into job assignments of members in their regions. Although the new system did not constitute an actual shift in power, it did create a new atmosphere of discussion and openness in regard to decision making. Discussion groups and working committees continued long after the renewal chapter ended and created a sense of membership involvement, responsibility, and excitement in the order's continuing process of renewal.

A new system of electing delegates to the general chapters was also instigated, based on age-group representation. Committees preparatory to general chapter were set up on a regional basis. The rationale underlying the regional system was greater collegiality and participation by the members in decisions that involved their daily lives.

During the renewal chapter a group of about thirty young nuns, all with only temporary vows in the order, began meeting to devise a proposal to establish an experimental local community that would be based on shared leadership rather than a centrally appointed local superior and consisted of nuns involved in various types of works. After much debate, the request was approved by the chapter delegates, and the first "superior-less" group was set up. Five young nuns—three with parish jobs directing youth and adult religious education programs, a nurse in a local public hospital, and a diocesan employee coordinating the religious vocation office—were group members. The traditional roles of the local superior such as conducting prayer and discussion sessions, determining the daily schedule of the members, making and overseeing a budget, and household maintenance were divided among the members. The experiment was considered a success by both those living there and the administration. Within a few years, other such communities were established, and eventually the model became the norm in the order.

Throughout the renewal process, one major change that occurred at all levels was consultation with interest groups as well as individual sisters regarding policies and decisions that affected them. Over a ten- to fifteen-year period, the hierarchical, authoritarian system gradually gave way to a more collegial, democratic system in which members gained an increasing voice in the order's affairs. The old system of assigning sisters to jobs without consulting or informing them before-hand was replaced with a process of discussion between the adminis-tration and the individual and often involved negotiation regarding the needs of the order and the desires of the individual sister. For a time, job openings in parish schools and religious education programs were advertised, and sisters were encouraged to make known their prefer-ences.

As more and more members wanted to leave the traditional class-room in parish schools and enter other professions such as adult reli-gious education, social work, allied health professions, law, and advocacy work, the order gradually allowed the nuns greater choice in regard to occupation even though the consequence was a severe crisis in personnel for parish schools. The consolidated, highly focused mis-sion of the order in terms of parochial school teaching and hospital work gave way to greater diversity and individualism in terms of occu-pational choice.

In the early years of renewal, the financial structure of the order received minimal attention. The members assumed that the order had sufficient resources to take care of them. Any notion of corporate responsibility or "open books" in regard to finances was not even raised. The financial naivete of the nuns was one of the last vestiges of the old system that remained. Early in the renewal process nuns began receiving an allowance for personal expenses (clothing, shoes, toilet articles, recreation) that replaced the old system of asking permission to take articles from a common closet. The allowance was minimal—first $25 per month and gradually increasing to $70—and, initially, a strict accounting of expenses was required to be submitted to the administration each year. Modest as this system was, it offered the beginning of personal financial accountability.

In addition to changes taking place within the order in the renewal process, many changes were also taking place on a national level in regard to religious orders of women; these changes likewise affected the Sisters of Service. Beginning with the Sister Formation Conference in the decade prior to the Council, several national coalitions of nuns formed with the purpose of mutual support as well as providing a voice for nuns in the Catholic Church. The most important of these groups was the Conference of Major Superiors of Women (CMSW, later renamed the Leadership Conference of Women Religious, LCWR), organized in 1956 as a national forum for the exchange of ideas and as a way to coordinate the professional, apostolic, and religious life of sisters. While the conference received formal approval of its statutes from Rome in 1959, over the decades there has been strain between the conference and the Vatican over a number of issues. In the mid-1960s CMSW sent a petition to Rome asking that nuns be represented on commissions dealing with the lives of sisters and received no reply, a reminder that the communication between Rome and the American sisters was meant to be one-way.

The conference, very supportive of renewal in religious orders, endorsed sisters' involvments in the Civil Rights Movement, petitioned "just salaries" for sisters, and in 1970 underscored its commitment to social justice by calling for a shift in priorities away from internal reorganization toward service to others. The decade of the 1970s was devoted to world solidarity, liberation themes, and women's issues (Quinonez and Turner, 1992).

During the late 1960s and early 1970s several clashes between the Vatican and specific religious orders of women in the United States focused attention on the relationship between religious orders and Roman authorities (see chapter 9 for detailed description of these events). Having been approached by fifteen or more religious orders also having difficulties with Rome, in 1984 LCWR set up mechanisms for establishing consultative panels so that no group of nuns could be forced to submit to official sanctions without recourse to the collaborative strength of American sisters. Although the panels had no formal authority, they did provide support to orders in conflict with Rome by organizing the collaboration of orders (Quinonez and Turner, 1992).

An example of such collaboration occurred when LCWR organized religious orders to protest the actions of Rome in condemning the nuns who signed a *New York Times* advertisement promoting free choice for women in regard to abortion. These actions indicated that American sisters were no longer willing to be docile servants without voice in matters that involved their well-being.

The struggles between CMSW and Rome over the decades display a new attitude toward the Vatican that has developed among sisters in this country, including many Sisters of Service. While valuing formal affiliation with Rome as an officially recognized religious order, during the process of renewal more and more sisters became less and less willing to accept a subservient position in the Church, as both women and nonclerics. Thus, the traditional subservience to Rome that characterized religious orders of women for centuries was being replaced with orders that wanted greater autonomy and dialogue with Church hierarchy.

Authority: 1990

In December 1989, the Sisters of Service received Rome's formal approval of their new constitution, a document that resulted from twenty years of experimentation with renewal in the order. The constitution states both the new conceptualization of religious life in the order and the renewed structures whereby the members of the order will live out their commitment.

New Meanings of Authority and Obedience

The new constitution places the vow of obedience in the context of an "attitude of openness to the providential plan of God for which we search in Scripture, in people, events, and circumstances, and in the inner workings of our own hearts." The document affirms that members live out trust in God within a specific community, the Sisters of Service, and that members search for God's will together and make decisions in the light of their corporate mission. By the vow of obedience, sisters commit themselves to obey those sisters who are entrusted with authority. However, authority is seen as furthering the basic values of interdependence and collaboration.

In the new ideas of authority and obedience there is a shift away from an identification of one person as the representative and interpreter of God's will to the idea that His will is manifested through the gifts and talents of all members in the community. The role of leadership is seen as integrating and focusing the multiplicity of gifts of community members, facilitating the response of members to the gospel and community goals, enabling and calling others forth, listening attentively to the times, and articulating a vision for the community in the contemporary world.

The notion of the entire community as responsible for the common good and corporate mission has developed. Replacing former responses of submission and blind acceptance of the mandates of others is commitment to engage with others in a search for the expression of God's will. A listening stance is seen as central to obedience: listening to the needs of the Church, the world, the congregation, insights of community members, including duly elected leaders and to one's own insights and experience.

In general, the sisters now reject attitudes of dependence, submission, subjection, and dominance over others and substitute the notion that consultation and communication are indispensable for the development of mature, responsible members who are committed to the goals and mission of the order.

New Structures of Leadership

With the 1987 general chapter a new system of authority was established in the order. The position of superior general was retained as the ultimate authority, but both the manner in which she is elected and the definition of her role changed significantly. Unlike the previous system in which chapter delegates nominated persons for the positions of superior general as well as the four general council seats, a new process operates. First, members in the order discuss extensively the qualities deemed necessary for each position. Second, members suggest names of people who seem to have these leadership qualities. If any person or group agrees on a name, then the central administration or a chapter planning committee makes contact with that individual and asks her to agree to be on a slate of candidates. The nominated individual is encouraged to "discern" whether she is willing to run for office. Those sisters who agree to be considered for office are invited to appear before the general chapter delegates for a speech outlining what gifts, as well as limitations, they feel they would bring to the position. The delegates then discuss the advantages and disadvantages of each candidate; a "listener" is present, and she reports the discussion to the candidate. Based on that feedback, each candidate has the option to either remain in the process or withdraw her name. The delegates then discuss each candidate and vote among those whose names remain.

The entire process operates on a model of "discernment," which means that God indicates His will for the order by speaking through the talents, personalities, and willingness of the candidates to serve in this capacity. In the 1987 election process, among the seventy-five original nominees for leadership positions, only thirteen chose to remain on the ballot for the final vote. In sharp contrast to previous elections, openness of discussion and the participation of the entire membership in the process characterized the new era.

The general chapter was also held on the main campus during summer months when the membership was gathered. Unlike the secrecy of previous chapters, most 1987 sessions were open to the membership. Although only the elected delegates could vote on issues, other members were present as listeners.

The constitution gives the superior general the power to admit to membership in the order, assign sisters to specific works, and function as the executive corporate officer of the order with the advice and consent of her council, but in practice she now operates consensually with her council. As the current Superior General states, "each of us brings a piece of the truth in order to arrive at the best decision we can. If one of us objects to a proposed decision, we discuss the issue to see if the dissenter can live with the decision. If not, we try to find an alternative option that each of us can live with."

The current council sees its role as threefold: (1) leadership implies keeping the vision and mission of the order always in mind; (2) administration deals primarily with the occupations and daily life-styles of members; and (3) corporate business of the order involves the financial dealings of the order, legal transactions, and determinations regarding the property and material holdings of the order as a corporation.

The superior general defines her role primarily in terms of the first function of articulating the vision and mission of the order in the world today. Rather than being involved in routine decisions regarding individual members or in the day-to-day operations of the order, she sees her first priority as challenging and encouraging the members to develop, and be committed to, a sense of mission for the order. Most of her communications to the members, therefore, are in the form of discussion materials, ideas to consider, proposals for greater participation and involvement of members in the affairs of the order, and the development of strategies to implement ideas and policies suggested by representative groups.

In 1973 the system of regional superiors was abolished and was supplanted with a system of clusters, with a member of the general council designated as the "contact person" for each cluster. A cluster consists of no more than twenty-five to thirty members, usually in geographical proximity, who meet together twice a year to discuss affairs of the order, generate issues for discussion at the annual convocation of members, and provide support and community for each other. As more and more sisters began to live alone, often geographically isolated from other members of the order, it was important to create smaller groups of sisters where camaraderie and a sense of communal belonging could be maintained. The prior regional system provided subgroups that were too large to accomplish this sense of *Gemeinshaft*. The smaller clusters serve as a substitute local community for sisters who live alone because of their work commitments.

The order established thirteen clusters in the United States and another in Mexico, the latter consisting of sixteen native Mexican nuns in the order. Each of the fourteen clusters in the order elects a leader who represents the cluster at the Representative Assembly, a group of sisters who constitute a liaison group between the central administration and the membership. The role of the council member in charge of each cluster is to maintain communication with each sister in her cluster, grant routine permissions for unusual expenditures, and discuss with individuals job placements, living situations, budgets, and continuing education. While issues of job changes and budgets require the formal approval of the council, the recommendations of the contact councillor are, in fact, almost always approved.

The Representative Assembly, consisting of the cluster representatives, meets twice a year to consider issues raised at the cluster level; it decides which issues warrant attention by the entire membership at its annual convocation. In effect, the assembly suggests agenda items for the upcoming annual meeting and assures that implementation of the resolutions from the previous meeting has been accomplished. The Representative Assembly also features a committee structure: liturgy (primarily planning for rituals to be used in the forthcoming annual meeting and at special congregational celebrations), vocation (recruitment), social justice, and investments. Each committee consists of members throughout the order and reports to the Representative Assembly.

The general assembly of members that meets for three to four days each summer has a number of functions, both instrumental and expressive. First, it is a time in which the membership comes together to experience themselves as a group dedicated to a common mission. The opening speech by the superior general focuses attention on the communal and corporate nature of the order and provides her the opportunity to articulate a vision for the order in the contemporary world. Her presence as leader of the group provides a ritual function of group identity and solidarity.

After the welcoming address by the leader, the members are recognized by each cluster rising and being presented by the elected representative of the cluster. Any sisters who are not present are acknowledged. Associate members, encouraged to attend the assembly meetings, are also recognized by each cluster.

The opening session of the assembly involves a well-prepared liturgical ritual, focused on the annual theme of the assembly. Typically, liturgical dance and drama are featured as well as the singing of songs about the order's founder, with music composed by an accomplished musician in the order. Throughout the days of assembly, liturgy and ritual play a central part in creating a sense of group identity.

The days are spent, in large part, in group discussion of topics organized by a committee that includes members of the Representative Assembly. The format consists of small, round-table discussions and then presentations of summaries to the entire assembly. As discussions proceed, issues of concern to the membership surface. There are also times of "open mike" during which any sister can stand before the group and express her opinion on any topic. By the final day of the assembly, it is obvious what the major concerns of the members are. In a final session, the organizing committee attempts to summarize the major issues and makes recommendations regarding solutions or policy implementation.

While the general assembly has no formal power to determine policy, it provides a vehicle for both communication among members as well as the expressive functions of group identity and commitment.

Resistance to Centralization in Religious Orders

The structures and meaning of authority as it developed over the past twenty-five years in religious orders make it clear that the pattern of centralization of authority that typically characterizes organizations in decline simply does not hold in this case. The question remains: Why not?

First, religious orders constitute a deviant case in terms of the usual centralization of authority within declining organizations because of the environmental milieu of the larger Church in which orders operate. The forces toward greater democratization and collegiality that swept the Church in the decades just prior to and during the sessions of Vatican II resulted in far-reaching changes within Church structures. The new ideology and theology that motivated these changes were both instigated by and, in turn, affected the systems of meaning and structure that developed within religious orders during the period of renewal.

With the rising levels of education of American nuns, the primary motivating force behind renewal was the nuns' desire for greater participation and voice in the system that affected their daily lives. Decentralization of authority, collegiality, and voice in decision making became the underlying themes and hallmark that directed renewal. Once the Vatican Council not only approved but also encouraged greater participation in decision making, even threats of organizational decline supplied an insufficient reason for most administrators to use centralization tactics to hold the organization together. Furthermore, such tactics simply were not feasible. Many American sisters would not have accepted them even if it meant defection from the institution. Therefore, the administrative option of centralizing authority under conditions of decline was not open to the leadership of religious orders.

CHAPTER 6

Loss of an Environmental Niche

Perhaps the greatest challenge that religious orders face today is that of defining their purpose or mission in contemporary society. Traditionally, in the United States religious orders, staffing parochial schools and Catholic hospitals, were valued by both Catholics and non-Catholics for their essential role in maintaining these institutions. With the ideological and structural changes initiated by the Second Vatican Council, as well as the decline in Catholic parochial schools, religious orders redefined their goals.

In the process of rewriting their constitutions, a task mandated by the Second Vatican Council, each order faces articulating the purpose of the order. For the first time in the two-hundred-year history of apostolic orders, many of them are having great difficulty grappling with the purpose that religious orders serve in the modernized Church. Many orders have substituted dedication to teaching and health-related work with the more nebulous goal of dedication to furthering the work of Christ in the world and/or serving the poor in society.

The anomie that exists in orders in regard to purpose stems from the individualism and diversity that exists in terms of members' occupations. As orders evolved from centrally structured, totalistic institutions into more democratic, voluntary organizations, members branched into all types of occupations, some of which are located outside the Church structure. The diversity of occupational settings has had consequences for the meaning of community and the forms of communal living for members. In this chapter, I contrast the purposes that religious orders served in the traditional Catholic Church with the ambiguity of purpose in today's Church as well as the impact of occupational diversity upon forms of communal life-styles.

The Mission of Traditional Religious Orders

The goal for the Sisters of Service, as stated in their 1947 constitution, exemplifies the stated purpose of almost every religious order in the United States at that time: "The primary end of the Institute is the sanctification of its members by the practice of the three vows of Poverty, Chastity, and Obedience, and the observance of these Constitutions. The secondary end is the Christian education and instruction of children and young ladies and the care of the sick." Noteworthy is the fact that the sanctification of members is the primary end with the good works of the order serving as a secondary goal. The philosophy behind this ordering of priorities is given in the second paragraph of the constitution which states that members are to acquire the virtues of religious living in order to "give edification everywhere by the sanctity of their lives" and to give children and young ladies a religious education and training in the fulfillment of their religious duties.

In terms of occupational commitments, the earlier constitutions made clear the fact that the order was committed to education and health care. As members were recruited into the order, they understood that they would be expected to be teachers or nurses. Because health care was always a minor organizational commitment in terms of the number of health care personnel among the members and the small number of health care facilities owned and/or operated by the order, the overwhelming thrust of the order was education, primarily within the Catholic parochial school system.

In the history of American Catholicism religious orders played a central role in the outstanding systems of education and health care provided by the Catholic Church. As historian James Hennesey (1981) notes, religious women have been valued in this country primarily as servants of the Church's institutions, especially the well-respected and strong Catholic educational system. Schools became, in his words, "one of the spinal cords around which religious life in the United States developed." The history of Catholic educational institutions in the United States parallels closely the history of religious orders in this country.

Many apostolic religious orders in the United States had been founded in Europe in the eighteenth and nineteenth centuries for the purpose of providing education, both religious and secular, to disadvantaged groups that did not have educational opportunities in the European school systems. The Sisters of Service, for example, began as a small group of Catholic girls who were taught to read and write and then sent out into the rural areas of France to teach local Catholic children the basics of literacy as well as fundamental Catholic doctrine.

As immigrant Catholic groups migrated to the land of opportunity in the United States, they tended to settle in ethnic enclaves around a Catholic church. In many instances, the immigrants built their own church and sent to their home community for a Catholic priest who spoke their language and understood their customs. The history of parishes as the basic organizational unit in the American Catholic Church is based on local groups of Catholic immigrants who used the local church not only for worship but also as a community organization that assisted them in the process of assimilation into American culture (Dolan, 1985).

The establishment of the Catholic parochial school system was a response to the emergence of the "common" or public schools that evolved in the 1830s and 1840s in this country. The public schools were rooted in a white, Anglo-Saxon, Protestant ideology that was basically intolerant of those outside this cultural milieu. Thus, for Native Americans, blacks, Jews, Catholics, Mormons, and people of other non-Christian religious heritages, the culture of the public schools was alien, often threatening to the language and religion of non–mainstream Protestant groups. By 1850 the Catholic bishops were denouncing the public schools as "both heretical and infidel" (Dolan, 1985). They saw the Protestant culture of the public schools, with their Protestant hymns, prayers, and Bible reading, as a threat to the religion of the Catholic children who attended.

By the 1850s the numbers of Catholics in the United States had increased significantly and constituted the largest single religious denomination in the country. The bishops felt the time had come to develop an independent Catholic educational system where Catholic children could be instructed in their religious heritage along with the knowledge and skills they needed to be part of American society.

In 1884 a convocation of American bishops voted to establish a parochial school in each parish. Pastors who did not comply within two years could be removed from duty; parish communities who did not support such a school would be reprehended by their bishop; and Catholic parents were obliged to send their children to parochial schools rather than to public schools.

A necessary prerequisite for the establishment of Catholic schools was the availability of teachers. The fact that the Church had available a large number of religious women who were able and willing to staff parochial schools was the major factor that explains the success of the parochial school system. In 1850 only about 1,344 nuns lived in the United States, but by 1890 the number had risen to 40,340 (Dolan, 1985). During the 1880s and 1890s many local pastors had returned to the home communities of the immigrants in their parishes explicitly seeking nuns to serve in the local parishes. Many pastors were successful in encouraging European orders to send three to four nuns to work in the new country. Once here, these pioneer nuns were able to recruit local girls to join them so that religious orders had begun to flourish by the turn of the century.

The willingness of nuns to work for low wages reduced the costs of maintaining Catholic schools and made feasible an otherwise financially impossible undertaking. By the early twentieth century, nuns generally received an annual salary of about $200, or one-third less than female public school teachers and one-half that received by teaching brothers (Dolan, 1985). To run the local convent and support the order, nuns relied on the services and goodwill of parishioners.

During the early decades of the twentieth century and continuing through the decade preceding the Second Vatican Council, young women joined religious orders in large numbers. Teaching was an attractive career for women, and most nuns were involved in teaching. Catholics also held religious life in high esteem so that it was not only socially acceptable but also admirable for a daughter to choose this vocation. For many women, especially those from the working class who could not afford advanced education, religious life offered a career that would have been difficult to attain outside the Church. Without this pool of available teachers, Catholic schools would never have been as numerous or successful as they were.

The Transition Years: Professionalizing Women Religious

The tumultuous period between World War II and the convocation of the Second Vatican Council (1945–1960) presented religious orders with organizational dilemmas that eventually led to the current demise that orders are experiencing. During those years religious orders confronted two forces that turned out to be incompatible in terms of rational organizational planning. First, the baby boomers born between the late 1940s and the early 1960s began reaching school age and created tremendous pressures for the establishment of more schools, first at the elementary level and then, eight years later, for high schools and later still for colleges. Between 1944 and 1949 the student population in parish elementary schools increased by nearly 450,000 (Byrne, 1990). During the next decade it grew 1,718,040, to a total of 4,195,781 in 1959, more than double its size at the end of the war. Parishes across the country added more than 2,400 new elementary schools.

While religious orders in the same period experienced a postwar boom in vocations, with the total number of religious women increasing by more than eleven thousand between 1945 and 1950, and more than twenty-one thousand during the following decade (a 21 percent increase), the Catholic student population grew by more than 200 percent in the same period. There were simply not enough nuns to fill the demand for parochial school teachers. Recruitment into religious orders took on a new urgency, and orders initiated all types of creative recruitment programs, including "aspirancies," special high schools for girls interested in joining the order. Moreover, rapidly rising costs of education made religious women even more desirable as teachers because of their willingness to work for low salaries. Religious orders had many more requests for teachers than they could possibly supply.

Concomitant with the boom in demand were the pressures for professionalization and credentialing of teachers. Many nuns were being sent into the classroom right out of high school with little or no college preparation. Because they were needed as teachers, nuns worked on college degrees in the summers. Many of them had fifteen to twenty years of teaching experience before they completed college degrees.

The pressures for credentialing came from both state educational agencies and voices within the Church itself. The Sister Formation Conference, established in 1954 as a group of religious women concerned about greater professionalization of religious women, began to put pressure on religious administrators to provide professional preparation for their members before sending them into either classroom or hospital. In 1950, Pope Pius XII added the voice of ecclesiastical authority to the need for professional preparation of nuns by instructing religious superiors to make sure that their members were on a par with their lay colleagues in terms of career readiness. At his urging, religious administrators in the United States complied; during the 1950s they began pulling nuns from the classroom and sending them to institutions of higher learning, both Catholic and secular universities.

The impact of this policy was enormous; its consequences were unanticipated by either the pontiff or the superiors who implemented it. In effect, nuns who had been cloistered and isolated for years, began to interact on a daily basis with lay people, men, women, Catholic, non-Catholic, married and single alike, in educational institutions across the country. As I argue elsewhere (Ebaugh, 1977), in the process of becoming professionalized, nuns began to shift their reference groups away from a totalistic, religious group of women like themselves to various kinds of alternative reference groups, including men, married women, and single women in careers. The defection of large numbers of nuns from religious orders during the late 1960s and throughout the 1970s can be traced, in part, to this shift in reference group orientation as nuns began to consider alternate life-styles (Ebaugh, 1977; San Giovanni, 1978).

The Impact of Vatican II
on Organizational Goals

The process of renewal and revitalization that followed the Second Vatican Council can be characterized as a movement away from a totalistic, autocratic, highly uniform organizational structure toward an emphasis upon greater individualism and respect for the needs and choices of individual members. The assignment of occupational careers and specific jobs for members gave way to a system in which the talents and desires of members were taken into account in terms of job preference. By the early 1970s fewer nuns were choosing traditional teaching careers in parochial schools and opting instead for other types of work, particularly what was known as "parish ministry."

With the Council's emphasis upon greater lay participation in the Church, parishes were establishing various types of jobs at the parish level to prepare and coordinate lay involvement in parish activities. Adult religious education classes mushroomed, and many nuns were hired to instruct the laity in "new theology" and the implementation of renewal in the Church. The process of soliciting and preparing converts to Catholicism also changed after the Council. The traditional system of making sure they memorized the Catholic catechism gave way to an elaborate structure of education and the mentoring of new converts, formalized in the Rite of Christian Initiation of Adults (RCIA) program. Catholic youth programs were also set up in parishes to provide a forum for discussion and social activities for teenagers and young adults in the Church. Because parochial schools were unable to accommodate the large numbers of baby boomers reaching school age in the 1960s and 1970s, those children who attended public schools were required to attend weekly Christian education classes in their parishes. Local churches were also more attuned to the social problems of their parishioners, and many provided social workers and counselors in outreach programs.

These burgeoning activities on the parish level produced a demand for personnel to coordinate and provide services. Because religious women were trained in modern theology, had teaching experience, and were willing to work for low salaries, again the nuns provided the personnel to run these parish programs. In addition, many younger nuns were disinterested in traditional parochial school teaching and wanted jobs they saw as more tied to the renewal movement occurring within the Church.

In addition to the expansion of nuns into parish work, they were also opting for various types of social work, both within and outside parish structures. The societal emphasis on the war against poverty, antihunger, and civil rights dovetailed with the theology of Vatican II that stressed the social responsibility of the Church in the modern world. By 1970 nuns were working in urban renewal programs, educational and advocacy work with migrants and poor people in Appalachia, alcoholism and drug counseling, university and seminary teaching, social work agencies, Head Start programs, the Job Corps, and Vista. Whereas in 1966, 63.7 percent of all professed nuns in the United States were involved in teaching and teaching administration, by 1982 the figure dropped to 29.1 percent (Neal, 1984).

This diversity in job settings for religious women was seen by many leaders in the Church as a positive outcome of the renewal process. In 1967 Sister Mary Luke Tobin, president of the Conference of Major Superiors of Women, wrote an essay on "The Mission of the Religious in the Twentieth Century," in which she said the contemporary world continues to require nuns' traditional works, but also needs their service for Catholics who are not reached by the present commitments of religious orders. Occupational diversity, therefore, was not only condoned by religious orders but also positively promoted as a way to extend the influence of nuns in the modern world.

Occupational diversity did not occur because religious orders formally reestabished their stated goals. Rather, the shift occurred informally as individual nuns requested reassignment to jobs outside the parochial school system. During the 1970s, the Sisters of Service, like many orders across the country, redefined job placement as the responsibility of the individual in consultation with the order, rather than assignment by the order to a particular job. Available jobs were advertized through the order's newsletter, in diocesan newspapers, and by word of mouth. Individuals interested in these jobs were encouraged to apply. As nuns were given greater choice in job assignment, fewer and fewer of them opted for traditional parochial school teaching.

In addition to the attrition of nuns from parochial schools into other types of work, the other factors that had an impact on the fate of parochial school personnel were the exodus of large numbers of nuns from religious orders and the declining numbers of Catholic girls entering religious orders. This decline in membership, coupled with the shift of religious women into nonteaching jobs, left the parochial schools facing a severe personnel problem. By 1985 the number of nuns teaching in Catholic schools was only 30,223, a 71 percent decline since 1965 (see figure 6.1). By 1984, 77 percent of the faculty in Catholics schools were lay teachers who required higher salaries than nuns had traditionally demanded (Byrne, 1990). As a result of the dwindling pool of religious women available to staff parochial schools, many of these schools were unable to survive. Between 1964 and 1984, 40 percent of the nation's Catholic high schools and 27 percent

FIGURE 6.1
Number of Nuns Teaching in Catholic Schools in the U.S. by Year

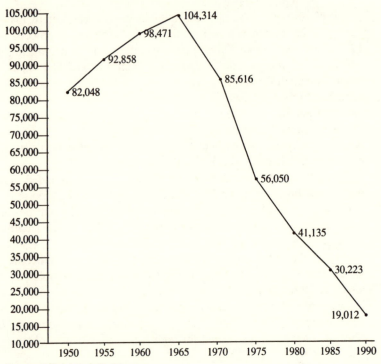

Source: *Official Catholic Directory.*

of its elementary schools closed their doors (*New York Times*, 1984; also *National Catholic Reporter*, 1982).

In addition, the "baby bust" of the late 1960s meant a significant decline in the numbers of children reaching school age. While Catholic birth rates, in the decades prior to the 1960s, tended to be higher than non-Catholic rates, from the mid 1960s on, the Catholic birth rate rapidly declined until it matched the national rate (Greeley, 1990). While Catholic parishes could hardly build sufficient schools to accommodate the baby-boomers born in the late 1940s and during the decade of the 1950s, by the late 1960s many of these school buildings stood empty.

Contemporary Organizational Anomie

In the process of renewal following Vatican II various factors, such as membership trends and greater individual choice of occupation, resulted in religious orders withdrawing from their traditional environmental niche within the parochial school system of the Church. The movement toward occupational diversity and individual job choice, however, makes it difficult today for orders to specify an alternative niche that would justify their uniqueness and function in either the modern Church or society. The organizational anomie that orders are feeling in regard to mission and purpose is perhaps the greatest challenge they are facing.

By the time of the 1987 general chapter, when the Sisters of Service was required to articulate its purpose for its new constitutions, the members found it difficult to agree on specific goals of the order, other than to posit very general aims that would encompass the varied works in which members were involved. Unlike the specific organizational purposes outlined in the 1947 constitution—dedication to the Christian education and instruction of children and young ladies and the care of the sick—the organizational goals posited in the revised constitutions are more general and nonspecific: "We are a community of women within the Church who dedicate our lives totally to furthering the mission of Jesus in our world. For the sake of our mission we are bound to one another in a common life by public profession of vows of poverty, celibacy, and obedience. We minister to people in need, finding light and strength in prayer and our communion with one another."

Even though the chapter delegates were able to agree on the above statement regarding the purpose or mission of the order, there was considerable discussion among the membership regarding the specific purpose of the order in the contemporary world. Many members were beginning to question the diversity in the order and asking whether diversity had gone too far in terms of organizational unity and impact in the world.

A phrase frequently used in conversation was "corporate mission" of the order. Many members were saying they were staying in the order, rather than opting to leave as many others had done, because they wanted to be part of the group's corporate mission, but they were unable to clearly articulate what that mission is.

Use of the term corporate mission indicates the fact that religious orders began to see themselves in more secular terms, that is, as organizations subject to the challenges and processes experienced by all types of organizations in society. Beginning in the 1970s, under the pressures of declining membership and dwindling financial resources, orders began hiring organizational consultants to assist them in organizational planning and restructuring. A major issue raised by these consultants was the articulation of clear organizational goals. Corporate mission represents the challenge from consultants to identify a new niche for orders in the contemporary world, a challenge that most religious orders are having difficulty in defining in a situation where members are committed to personal career goals. The Sisters of Service, like most orders, has tended to redefine its mission in very broad terms to accommodate the diversity of occupational choices.

Periodically over the past few years, small groups of members have suggested that the order reconstitute its mission by selecting a disadvantaged group in the society and/or a geographical area and concentrating the activities of its members toward bettering the social conditions of this group or region. However, while the idea appeals to some members, the vast majority are unwilling to give up their present commitments for such a cause. It is obvious that the spirit of individualism has become deeply rooted within the order and that it has become virtually impossible to return to any structure that resembles centralization or uniformity. A number of the nuns whom I interviewed made it clear that any move away from individualism toward greater uniformity among members would result in their leaving the order. As one member put it, "If the administration insisted that we live in large communities again or that everyone has to do the same kind of work, I would leave. That would be indicative of regression and restricting individual choices."

The Sisters of Service has defined its corporate mission as dedication to furthering Christ's kingdom on earth, especially among the materially poor, by using financial resources in a socially responsible way. This mission has been implemented by investing funds in companies that are socially responsible and by supporting several endeavors of members who are involved with the materially disadvantaged, such as a foster home to care for babies with AIDS. Such efforts, however, are removed from the daily activities of most members.

The order, therefore, faces a dilemma: one way to avert organizational demise is to recapture an environmental niche for the organization, some specific function in society or the Church that can best be served by the specific organization. Given the ethos of individualism that has been allowed to develop in the order, the attempt to centralize activities toward a specific group or population will be met with resistance and probably defection of some members from the group. Yet, the failure to focus on a common cause produces a sense of anomie for many group members. The result for religious orders in this predicament is an organizational dilemma that probably will result in the eventual demise of the order.

Shifts in Meaning of Community

Occupational diversity within religious orders has had an impact upon communal life-styles of members as well as the way in which members define community. In both traditional as well as contemporary orders, a distinguishing feature of religious life has been commitment to being part of a community of women in the Church. This feature of living in community, coupled with commitment to the three vows of poverty, chastity, and obedience, distinguishes members of a religious order from committed lay people in the Catholic Church. However, what it means to "live in community" for today's nuns is quite different from community living prior to the Council. A major cause for the shift in meaning can be traced to the changes that occurred in terms of occupational diversity among members.

In the traditional system of religious life, assignment to a specific job implied assignment to a specific living situation since the members who worked together in a given school or hospital lived together, usually in a facility provided by the parish. Each local community, usually consisting of two to fifteen people, had the common goal of staffing a local school or hospital. Members engaged in professional work during the day, but they were expected to return to their local convents after work hours to pray and socialize with their community.

Local communities were replicas of the larger order in terms of goals, life-style, and authority structure. Each house had an appointed local superior who represented the superior general, as well as a daily schedule that was approved by the superior general. In terms of daily routines, as well as rules and regulations that governed the operation of each local community, there was little variation. Even though members were involved in professional activities during the day and interacted with students, parents, patients, and coworkers in the course of these activities, their after-work hours followed the model of the cloister that characterized religious orders prior to the Council. Exposure to the media, telephone calls, visiting with outsiders, and trips to doctors' offices, and visits with family and friends were regulated by the local superior. Salaries were sent directly to the motherhouse, and expenses of the local house were paid by the superior or treasurer of the local house from a check sent by the motherhouse each month. Other than the local superior or treasurer, the nuns had no involvement with money. Their needs were taken care of in terms of room and board, as well as clothing and necessary medical expenses. The uniform habit of nuns in each order made it easy to identify members and signaled to laity the limits of social interaction. The habit was an essential part of the cloister that characterized nuns in the traditional Church and set them apart from ordinary lay people.

Even though nuns were involved in active ministries in the Church, such as teaching and hospital work, their life-style prior to the renewal of Vatican II was still very much cloistered, in terms of both the physical isolation of their local convents and, especially, the social isolation demanded by the rules of convent living. Because they associated primarily with other nuns in their local convent and were highly regulated by rules of the order, nuns were constantly reminded that they were set apart from society and belonged to a community dedicated to spiritual goals. The local community was the vehicle through which members were tied to the larger order. Because each community was highly uniform in life-style and demands upon members, there was a heightened sense of belonging to the order. Awareness of belonging to a religious order, with its unique history and commitment to particular types of service in the Church, was part of daily living for members. It was impossible, in the traditional system, not to be constantly reminded of one's religious identity.

As occupational diversity occurred in religious orders, two things happened in terms of local communities. Nuns began to leave the parochial schools for broader parish work as well as work outside parish settings; in the early years they tended to live in local communities of nuns still working in Catholic schools. Local communities, therefore, consisted of many members who were still working in parochial schools and one or two members who were doing other types of work. Frequently, such other work demanded unusual hours such as night meetings, late afternoon work, and weekend involvement. It was difficult, if not impossible, for the nontraditional nun to be present at community prayer and communal activities. Nuns in new works also tended to have the use of their own car, provided by either the parish in which they worked or the order. They also tended to have financial needs different from the teaching nuns because of continuing education demands, meals eaten away from the community, and social activities demanded by the job. As more and more nuns became involved in nontraditional careers, the uniformity of local community life gave way to greater diversity in daily routines, finances, and rules regulating social contact.

By the mid 1970s more nuns were accepting jobs in geographical areas where there were no established local communities of the order. Some of these individuals began living with nuns of other orders, and others were allowed to live in rented houses or apartments, either alone or with another member of the order who was working in the same geographical area. In addition to accepting jobs in areas where there were no other members of the order, by the late 1970s some nuns were being allowed to live alone because they felt they either needed such an experience for personal growth or preferred an individual life-style to communal living.

As more and more nuns lived outside traditional local communities—alone, with one other member of the order, or with members of other orders—the order established the regional governmental structure described in chapter 5. In addition, the Sisters of Service began a newsletter to inform members of collective issues facing the order, news of important events concerning members as well as their families, potential recruits interested in joining the order, job openings in dioceses and parishes, and items of general interest to the membership. Routinely, in an effort to reaffirm organizational history, the newsletter presented a life history of one older member. In addition, a telephone relay line was established whereby members informed one another of important events, especially serious illness and death of members. In addition, good friends in the order frequently call one another; telephone bills constitute a major portion of many members' monthly personal allowances. All these efforts represented an attempt to nurture a sense of group belonging under conditions where members do not see one another on a daily basis.

During the decade of the 1970s, the general assembly held at the motherhouse each summer also became the highlight of congregational activity. Each member was expected to attend. In addition to conducting organizational business and informing members of policy changes and the financial status of the order, the gathering takes the form of a group celebration. Liturgical prayer and ritual are central to the gathering as are social activities. The general assembly is the focal point in reminding members of their communal association as well as the organizational history that they all share.

Despite the diversity of occupations and living situations of members, my interviews with members in the Sisters of Service indicate that most people have a strong sense of identity with the community. They no longer identify with local communities, but members place great value in belonging to an organization that values Christian virtues and a commitment to living a spiritual life. This sense of sharing basic values, especially of a religious nature, encourages members not only to remain in the order but also to be enthusiastic about their identification with the order. Many of those I interviewed said they were proud to be associated with a group of women dedicated to living a life of prayer and Christian witness. For example, one member said, "It feels good to be connected to a group that articulates values of social justice and Christian living that I believe in. It is stimulating to belong to a group that is committed to ideals. There is so much selfishness in the world today that I like being part of a group that thinks beyond just what makes me happy." Another interviewee expressed it in more theological terms: "I believe in the reason we are nuns in the first place, that is, to give witness to a Provident God and to religious values in the world. I like being part of a group whose main purpose is to remind people that God is real and that He is alive in our world today."

The majority of those I interviewed feel closely associated with the order even under conditions where they might not see another member of the order for weeks at a time. Community, for them, is maintained by the memory of having been socialized in the order with a group of women who share basic values, experiences, and history in the order. As one person who goes weeks without seeing another member put it,

"I am a Sister of Service, through and through, and cannot imagine myself any other way. We all share a history."

Although older members maintain a strong identification with the group, there seems to be greater ambivalence on the part of younger ones. A major reason for the difference between age groups can be traced to their different socialization experiences. Nuns over forty were socialized in the traditional system in which they went through formation with a large cohort and were relatively isolated from people outside the order. The socialization process was characterized by many of the commitment-building mechanisms recognized in the sociological literature, such as strong boundaries between insiders and outsiders, mortification rituals whose purpose was to lead to a rebirth of the recruit in a new spiritual identity, abstinence from normal pleasures of the body, and sacrifice. As Kanter's (1972) research shows, the above mechanisms are powerful in creating commitment to group values and goals. In addition, the fact that a large number of individuals went through the process together created both consensual validation of what was being taught and a sense of solidarity among those going through the process. Nuns who are younger than forty had a very different socialization experience. Not only were they less isolated from outsiders during the process and had greater individual freedom, but they were also isolated in terms of the size of cohort going through the experience. Entering classes dropped in size from eight to ten among those who are now thirty to forty to classes of one or two in most recent years. Socialization is no longer a group phenomenon, in terms of either numbers or uniformity in the process.

In summary, the decline in Catholic parochial schools in the United States, along with the theological changes initiated by the Second Vatican Council, lead to the loss of the traditional environmental niche that religious orders had for centuries filled in the Church and in society. As nuns began to branch out into a diversity of occupations, both within and outside Church institutions, it became more and more difficult to pinpoint exactly what function nuns serve in the Church and, concomitantly, what constitutes their corporate goal and mission. While many orders have redefined their goal in more general terms, such as social justice or witnessing to Christian values, these amorphous goals are insufficient to create a strong sense of purpose in religious orders.

CHAPTER 7

Recruitment and Retention

Both the primary cause of organizational decline in religious orders and the perceived hope for the future lies in their recruitment and socialization structures. The fact that few new members are joining the vowed ranks of orders is the primary factor driving up the median age of members. At the same time, the new associate member programs that many orders have initiated as a part of "formation" represents the hope for the future for many members in orders today. In this chapter I describe the significant changes that have occurred in the recruitment and socialization program of the Sisters of Service, as well as the development of their associate member program—the phoenix of hope for many members.

Changing Demographics of New Members

In the two decades prior to Vatican II the Sisters of Service, like most religious orders, experienced the largest increase in new members in its history. Entering cohorts ranged between twenty and thirty each year. In 1955, for example, twenty-three young women entered; in 1960, the number rose to thirty. By the decade of the 1970s, however, the number of new recruits began to steadily decline, coming to a virtual halt during the 1980s. In 1982, for example, the order admitted one new candidate, had one novice in training, and had only two young women actively interested in joining. Moreover, there were only seven members with temporary vows, compared to more than twenty times that number just ten years earlier. During the 1980s the situation did not improve but remained at a steady state. In 1989–1990 the order had no novice in formation, and only one young woman was in the initial formation stage.

Interestingly, however, the above statistics reflect entrance data for the order headquartered in the United States, but the small formation program located in Mexico continued to grow throughout the decades. While recruits were dwindling in this country, the number of young women entering the Mexican branch grew. In 1990 they had one novice, four in the prenovitiate stage, and two who planned to enter shortly. Given the branch's small size—only sixteen vowed members—the rate of recruitment was relatively high. The fact of growth in Mexico at the same time that the U.S. order experienced drastic decline in recruits supports my argument, to be elaborated, that there exists a relationship between opportunities for female mobility in a society and rates of recruitment.

What explains the drastic reduction in the number of young women interested in entering a religious order? I contend that three major factors explain the decline in recruits: (1) changes in the opportunity structure available to young women in an advanced industrial society; (2) decline of the parochial school system that served as the recruiting base for religious orders; and (3) changes in age requirements for recruits.

Unlike rural societies or third world countries where joining a convent provides upward mobility in terms of educational and occupational opportunities, in the United States today women have the opportunity to obtain an education and professional jobs. In addition, for those women with altruistic aspirations, various avenues are open for activism. If the aspiration is humanitarian rather than religiously inspired, then the Peace Corps, Vista, some civil service jobs, and social work are viable options. In the event that a young woman is religiously motivated and wants to be involved in religious work, there are opportunities today on both Catholic diocesan and parish levels, for full-time employment as well as volunteer work.

None of the above options requires the costs of renouncing either a sexual life or a family. As career opportunities and church work opened up for women, the costs of celibacy outweighed the unique rewards previously associated with religious status in the Church (Ebaugh, 1977). Prior to the Council, not only did religious life provide a unique avenue for education and a career for women, but it also conveyed a privileged status in the Catholic Church. The document on religious life that resulted from the Second Vatican Council made it clear that nuns were not part of the clerical ranks in the Church but, because of their baptism and confirmation, were part of the laity. With the extinction of religious garb and the demise of cloistered structures for nuns, the rewards of "set apartness" and special honor were eradicated. Celibacy, under these conditions, was not counterbalanced with the rewards previously associated with the status of nun.

In addition, as religious orders expanded their mission and fewer nuns taught in parochial schools, their recruiting base shifted. During the 1950s and 1960s, most new recruits came from Catholic grammar and high schools in which the nuns taught. For many girls in these schools, the nuns were the most educated and only professional women they knew. In addition, their unusual, cloistered life-style, along with admirable religious ideals, gave a sense of awe and inspiration to young women who were idealistic and searching for a meaningful future. During the 1970s and 1980s, there was a drastic decline in the numbers of religious women teaching in parochial schools, as discussed earlier. There were also fewer Catholic girls being educated in parochial schools. Thus, the "captive audience" of young Catholic girls who were highly influenced by their religious women teachers no longer existed. As a result, the natural recruiting base was gone. The declining birth rate that affected Catholics, as well as non-Catholics, beginning in the mid 1960s and extending to the present, also reduced the pool of potential recruits.

In addition to recruiting in parochial high schools, during the early 1950s many religious orders, including the Sisters of Service, opened aspirancies in their own motherhouses. Aspirancies were high schools for girls who were interested in joining the order after high school graduation. These order-related high schools were usually established in conjunction with a local Catholic high school run by the order. Girls in the aspirancy attended some classes along with students in the local high school. However, they also had many of their own classes, usually taught by highly qualified nuns in the order. These elite high schools aimed to provide a top-notch education for their students, along with instruction in Catholic theology as well as the history and goals of the order.

Many girls who entered the aspirancy came from small, rural communities where educational opportunities were limited, or from immigrant, urban communities where they were not exposed to lay role models of upwardly mobile women. The opportunity to receive a quality education, along with the opportunity to explore the viability of a religious vocation as a nun, appealed to these Catholic girls. Because the order subsidized the aspirancy, it was also a way to receive a quality education that might otherwise have been impossible.

The aspirants, as they were called, lived during the academic year as a group, usually at the motherhouse of the order. They spent holidays and summer vacation at home with their families, but during the time they spent together they were not allowed to date and, except for class time, were virtually isolated from people outside their group. In many ways, by following the life-style of nuns in the order they were given a taste of what it would be like to be a member in the order. Approximately half of those who attended the aspirancy proceeded to the next step of candidacy in the order. Likewise, about half of those who entered the order each year were former aspirants and half came from various high schools where the nuns taught.

In terms of a recruiting base, the aspirancy provided an ideal opportunity to encourage those already interested in religious life to pursue that option. Aspirants were also frequently used to recruit girls from other high schools. They would accompany the nun recruiter to give talks in high schools where nuns in the order taught. During the summer, aspirants also helped run "vocation workshops," week-long retreats for eighth grade and high school girls interested in joining the order.

Aspirancies were commonplace in religious orders during the 1950s and 1960s. However, by the early 1970s most orders, including the Sisters of Service, had discontinued them because of the shift that occurred in terms of the type of recruit sought by orders.

The third factor that explains the decline in recruits is primarily the shift in age requirements that the order instituted in the 1970s. Prior to that time most recruits were in their teens, having just completed their high school education. For example, in 1965 twenty of the twenty-five who entered had completed high school, and only five had completed some college. By 1980 the order had changed its entrance requirements to accept only women who had completed some college or had at least one year of work experience. The shift in requirements resulted from the idea that living a religious life must be a mature choice, made only after the individual has had some experience with independent living outside the convent. As a result of the change in requirements, applicants today tend to be in their twenties and early thirties, to have been in college or held a job for several years, to have dated, owned a car, and been financially independent. It is much more difficult to locate and attract this older, more experienced pool of candidates than it was in the parochial school system where potential recruits were much younger, more impressionable, less experienced, and in daily contact with their nun teachers.

Recruitment and Socialization in the Traditional System

It is possible to present a general portrait of the type of individual who entered religious orders in the era prior to Vatican II. The recruit typically came from a strong Catholic family who was not only supportive but also honored to have a daughter "chosen by God" for special service in the Church. Not only her immediate family, but her extended family, as well as the local Catholic community, treated her with respect and honor once she entered the convent.

The typical recruit was in her late teens, a recent graduate from either the aspirancy of the order or a Catholic high school run by the order. She tended to have close friendship ties with professed members of the order who were her role models during high school. In addition, the recruit frequently knew others who entered the order with her or in the recent past. She was, therefore, entering a group with whom she already had many social ties.

Given the low rates of divorce in traditional Catholic families, as well as the emphasis on family solidarity among Catholic immigrant groups, the recruit usually came from a relatively stable family. Moreover, having grown up in a traditional Catholic family and having gone to a Catholic high school, she tended to have conservative moral values.

Most recruits came from rural areas, small town communities, or urban immigrant communities in which few women worked outside the home. Educational and professional opportunities were almost nonexistent for these women. Therefore, going to college was simply not an option for many of those who entered religious orders.

In addition, prior to the mid 1960s there were few outlets for young

girls who were idealistic and wanted to get involved in either humanitarian or social justice work. The Peace Corps, Vista Workers, and the
numerous social movements of the late 1960s were not yet available to
these girls. Spurred on by the idealism portrayed by their nun teachers,
those who wanted to "help people" and better conditions for the disadvantaged in the world saw religious life as the only viable option.

Once the recruit entered an order, she went through a carefully defined and regimented series of stages in the process of becoming a full-
fledged, vowed member of the order. Upon entering, along with a
cohort of twenty to thirty others of about the same age and inexperi-
ence, the recruit was known as a candidate. Secular clothes were exchanged for a black uniform, a modified version of the nun's habit,
with a floor length skirt and long sleeved blouse. Candidates lived
together at the motherhouse with their own assigned dormitory, study
hall, and dining area with a superior assigned by the mother general.
Like the vowed members, they rose at 5:00 a.m. and were expected to
be in chapel for morning prayer and Mass by 5:25. After prayer and
breakfast, they attended college classes, as a group, but with lay students at the college on the motherhouse campus. Meals, recreation,
and study time were scheduled by the superior and done as a group.
Family members were permitted to visit once a month, and candidates
were allowed to go home for a week's visit during the summer. However, they were required to wear their candidate's uniform while home
and to "act as befitting one who is seeking religious life."

During her second year of college classes, a candidate's behavior
and progress was evaluated by the mother general and her council;
those who passed the test were permitted to progress to the next step,
becoming a postulant. In a church ceremony, the postulant was cer-
emoniously given "the cape," the first piece of a nun's habit. The six
months as a postulant were spent anticipating the time at which the
person would be accepted into the novitiate, the cloistered year the
recruit would spend in prayer and study of the religious vows she
would take at the end of her novitiate year.

The ceremony of acceptance into the novitiate was the time at which
the postulant entered the church dressed as a "bride of Christ" and
during the ceremony exchanged her worldly garb for the habit of the
nun and the traditional rosary. Both the habit ceremony and the exchange of her baptismal name for that of Sister (followed by a Catholic
saint's name) were symbolic of the death and rebirth process she was

expected to experience psychologically. The ceremony was witnessed by family and friends and was often celebrated like a wedding in the family.

The cloistered year of the novitiate, in which the novice took only theology and philosophy classes and suspended involvments with anyone outside her novitiate group, culminated with her professing the three vows of religious life—poverty, chastity, and obedience, for one year at a time. Upon pronouncing her vows for the first time, she became an annual professed member of the order, repeating vows annually for six years. After this probationary period, her behavior and attitudes were reevaluated by the administration to determine whether she would be allowed to pronounce final vows in the order. During her years as an annual professed member, the recruit completed her college education and engaged in the active works of the order.

Recruitment and Socialization Today

The recruitment and socialization process is very different today. Unlike "vocation recruiters" in the traditional system—that is, sisters who traveled to the parochial schools in which members taught and invited young girls to join the order—today each member is asked to try to identify women they work with who might be interested in religious life. However, this system is unproductive, primarily because of lack of interest on the part of potential recruits who are older and already in the work force. In addition, more and more members in the order are beginning to question whether it is wise and ethical to encourage young women to enter an organization that has no future.

The few women who are entering religious orders today are very different from those who entered in an earlier era. First, only older women with at least some college or work experience are accepted. Implicit in this requirement is the probability that these women have had dating experience, some degree of financial independence, and have lived apart from their families for a time. Many recruits have not attended Catholic high schools and have had less contact with nuns than in the earlier era. Contact with nuns is frequently made at the parish level where they have worked with a nun in parish activities. In other cases, recruits have met nuns through their work and have become friends with them.

Given the dissolution of many Catholic immigrant communities in the United States and the increased urbanization of society, most contemporary recruits come from urban areas and communities that are not predominantly Catholic. Likewise, they do not have the support or esteem of home communities that characterized recruits in the traditional system. Being a nun today does not garner the same social status and respect that it did earlier, among either Catholics or non-Catholics.

Those entering religious orders today have not been immune from the social ills of contemporary society, including the increasing number of people from dysfunctional families. The prevalence of divorce, of living in stepfamilies, of experiencing sexual and physical abuse, and witnessing the problems related to drug and alcohol abuse within families is as characteristic of recruits into religious life as they are of other societal members. As a result, formation programs today are having to deal with the psychological problems and scars suffered by people growing up in these kinds of family situations. The agendas of national meetings of formation directors reflect this need. The issue of dysfunctional family problems of new recruits has become a major issue at these meetings.

Perhaps the major difference between recruits today and those who entered religious orders prior to Vatican II is a shift in the reasons why young women join. Previously, the desire to be of service to people, whether as teachers, nurses, social workers, or missionaries in foreign countries, constituted the major motivation for entering a convent. Today recruits express their purpose not so much in terms of service but in terms of community; that is, they seek to fulfill personal needs of belonging to a meaningful group that shares similar values, especially those of Christian living. Unlike the outward focus of earlier eras, today's recruits seem more focused upon personal spiritual development.

When an individual expresses an interest in knowing more about the order, she is invited to become an "affiliate," the first step in the new socialization process. Affiliates remain in their jobs, continue their independent living arrangements, are self-supporting but have contact with both the director of formation and a local community of Sisters of Service. They are invited to participate in prayer and social activities with members in their geographical area, to be part of regional cluster meetings, and to attend the annual general assembly of the order. There is no formalized program that the affiliates follow; rather, in consultation with the formation director in the order, they work out an individualized program to learn more about the order and to nourish a spiritual life that motivates them to consider membership in the order. In recent years, the order has had four to five affiliates at any given time.

If and when the affiliate, along with the formation director, decides that she is serious about becoming a member of the order, she is accepted into the prenovitiate program. Until a year ago, the recruit was required, at this stage, to relocate to a central formation center and find a job in the vicinity. However, for the first time in 1990, the order accepted an older, divorced woman into the prenovitiate program and allowed her to live with a local community of the Sisters of Service in the city where she had both a job and a family. A member in the local community was appointed as her "mentor," a substitute for the traditional formation director. In addition to relaxing the requirement to relocate for the prenovitiate stage, the acceptance of the first divorced recruit also poses new challenges in terms of financial and social responsibilities for her nuclear family.

Unlike the traditional system in which recruits were socialized as part of a cohort, today they tend to go through the stages alone. As a result, the mechanism of strong solidarity and identification with a cohort is no longer possible, and it is more difficult to establish a peer group within the order. In an attempt to provide peer support, the Sisters of Service have joined with several other religious orders, both male and female orders, to establish an intercongregational formation program. At both the prenovitiate and novitiate stages, recruits meet weekly with those from other orders to pray together, discuss issues of religious life, and socialize. A consequence of the intercongregational program is that male and female recruits not only interact regularly but engage in deeply personal discussions regarding life values and goals. Although there has been no known case of defection from the order because of romantic involvments, several recent recruits expressed romantic attractions to male members of the group.

The prenovitiate stage of formation usually lasts a year. The recruit, in consultation with the formation director, works out personal goals that she wants to achieve before moving to the next stage. Many of these goals relate to spiritual growth and to learning more about the way religious life is lived out in the Sisters of Service.

At the point at which the recruit, along with the formation director and superior general of the order, decides that she is ready to move on to the novitiate, she is accepted as a novice in the order in a simple prayer ceremony. Gone is the image of the bride, the birth and rebirth ceremonies, and the elaborate bestowal of the habit and new name that characterized the former investiture ceremony. Today her family and friends may not even be there; rather, a few members of the order are present, along with the administrators who formally admit her into the order.

During her two years of novitiate, the novice lives at the Formation House, often the only person in formation. Along with the formation director, several members of the order who work in the area also share the living facility and constitute a local community. The novice interrupts her working career for the two years that she is in the novitiate. For the first year she attends theology classes, studies the religious vows, and engages in some type of volunteer church work, such as parish work, a hospice program, volunteer hospital work, or caring for the aged. During her second year she has a "mission experience"; that is, she spends time in a setting in which members of the order are working.

After her novitiate years, and with mutual agreement between the novice and the administration, she makes first vows in the order and becomes an "annual professed" member, a status she holds for three to nine years until she makes final vows. Again, there is no set period for the stage of annual vows; rather, the individual, along with the administration of the order, decides if and when she is ready for a permanent commitment.

Associate Membership

In 1984 the Sisters of Service followed the lead of many other religious orders in the United States and initiated an associate member program. At the same time that recruitment to a vowed life in the order has come to a virtual standstill, the associate program has mushroomed faster than the order can accommodate. There are currently more than 150 associate members in the Sisters of Service.

Associate members are Christian, not necessarily Catholic, men and women who want to share in the goals and spirituality of the Sisters of Service without becoming vowed members. They tend to be religiously committed laity who want a deeper and more involved religious life than they are able to find in parishes. Many of them have been associated with the Sisters of Service as former members, students, coworkers, or members of a nun's biological family.

Associates were initially invited into membership by a vowed member in the order. Within the first year, more than forty men and women were accepted as associates. Many of these new members were so enthusiastic about their experience that they asked to be allowed to recruit others. Many current associates were drawn into the program by fellow associates who found their experience valuable and rewarding.

The associates sign an agreement with the order as part of an induction ceremony, but they have no financial commitments to the order. Likewise, the order has no financial or legal commitments to the associates. The associate program, therefore, is clearly not an effort to remedy the order's financial situation. Rather, it is an attempt to share the mission of spreading Christ's kingdom in light of the history and spirit of the particular order. This goal is expressed by the term "sharing the charism" of the order, indicating the unique character and Christian virtues that characterize each religious order and give it uniqueness. Sharing in the charism of the order is the primary goal stated throughout the Sisters of Service's literature on the associate membership program.

Associates receive all information sent to vowed members, participate in regional cluster meetings, are invited to general assembly, and serve on various congregational committees. They have also raised the possibility of having representation in the administrative structure, namely, the Representative Assembly of the order.

A board of directors governs the associate program; it includes representatives from the vowed members and the associates. The purpose of the board is to make recommendations regarding the program.

The associate membership program is serving positive functions for both the associates and the order. Comraderie and the opportunity for a support group that shares basic Christian values are the major outcomes for the associates. In addition, being part of a group mission is energizing for many associates who are committed to the values and work of the Church. For the order, the associates provide several functions. Most important, the growth and vitality of the program gives hope and the possibility of a future to an organization that must look realistically at its diminishing membership and financial condition. The flourishing associate program provides a possibility for the rising of the phoenix in terms of a new form of religious life through which the history and charism of the order can be passed on to new generations.

Second, the associates provide new perspectives and challenges for many vowed members who take religious life in its present form for granted. By their questions and remarks, the associates frequently challenge the members to explain the meaning and relevance of their lives as nuns. The associates, many of them professional men and women, also bring a real-life, practical perspective to many discussions that go on within the order. Especially in the areas of finance and business, the associates often challenge policies and plans.

Although the associate program is currently serving the needs of both the associates and the order, it is clear that the program depends upon the core vowed members for inspiration, direction, and enthusiasm. Many vowed members in the order hope that the associates could one day provide their own leadership and core, but it seems highly unlikely that this would happen and extend the life of the order for any length of time. The associates have not experienced the kind of intense socialization into religious life that the vowed members have, nor do they have the financial and group commitment to the order. After all, by the nature of their membership they remain independent in terms of marital status, job, finances, and family commitments. Unlike the vowed members, their lives are not totally defined in terms of the order's future. They are valuable adjuncts to the core, vowed membership, but it is doubtful that the program could survive the demise of the order.

Member Defections

Like religious orders throughout the United States, the Sisters of Service lost very few vowed members prior to the opening of the Vatican Council in 1963. Between 1950 and 1963, for example, thirteen people in annual vows decided not to proceed with a permanent commitment; however, no one with perpetual vows left the order. In 1963 thirteen with annual vows left, along with three who had already made final vows. Between 1966 and 1981 the order lost 116 members, with the largest numbers leaving in 1970. In that year alone nineteen members defected, including ten permanently vowed members.

Although I did not conduct systematic interviews with former members of the Sisters of Service, conversations with several who had left, as well as information provided by various current members in the order, indicates that leavers followed the patterns I found in my earlier study of ex-nuns (Ebaugh, 1977). In that study, I interviewed twenty ex-nuns who had left each of three case study orders: in terms of change a liberal order, a conservative order, and a moderate order. Reasons for leaving each type of order varied. Those leaving the liberal order felt that the uniqueness and rewards of religious life were no longer sufficient to justify the costs of celibacy, and those who wanted to do service work within the Church saw opportunities within the parish structure. The leavers from the conservative order voiced dissatisfaction with the lack of change in the order as their primary reason for leaving.

The Sisters of Service were rated a moderate change order on the basis of their change score in my earlier study. The reasons for members leaving the order paralleled those of exiters from the moderate change order in that study. Specifically, they left for more personal reasons rather than for reasons related to the degree and nature of organizational change. Many leavers expressed a similar scenario. They entered along with a large cohort of other new recruits, which provided strong consensual validation of the life-style. They were told that they were being blessed with a special calling to religious life, one they should not question. They experienced substantial status rewards in both their Catholic families and the Catholic communities from which they came. For years they did not question their vocation, even though many of them were unhappy. The events of Vatican II and the Council's mandate for the reevaluation of the outdated structures of religious life meant that each nun was involved in the renewal process and challenged to evaluate her own commitment. This provided those who wanted other opportunities and life-styles the opportunity and the justification for exiting.

The majority of those who exited were younger members who had not yet built up enough investments in the order to make exiting too costly. Many were still annually professed and in their twenties, although others were full-fledged members in their thirties and early forties. The loss of approximately 15 percent of the order was less significant than the demographics of those who left, namely, members of the younger cohorts. The simultaneous decrease in new recruits resulted in the dramatic rise in median age of members in the order within a relatively few years.

Retention: Why Stay?

My earlier book on change in religious orders (Ebaugh, 1977) focused upon structural changes and their impact upon rates of exiting. I was interested in why people were leaving religious orders. Given the demographic changes that such groups have experienced in the past twenty years and the probability of their demise in the future, the intriguing current question is why younger members, with viable alternatives, are staying and why some, albeit very few, young women are entering.

I interviewed thirteen women in the Sisters of Service, aged thirty to sixty-five, all of whom had been in the order for twelve or more years and had viable job opportunities outside the order. Eight of them, involved in professional careers, were making salaries comparable to their lay counterparts. None of the twelve was living in traditional local communities, but each was living either alone in an apartment or with one other member of the order. Given their ages, their professional involvements, and their substantial salaries compared with many others in the order, these women represent the future of the order.

My major interview question to this group was: Why do you stay? The response I got, without exception, was a version of: Why not? Here is a typical response given by one woman: "The order is my family, we have a history together. It is home, family, friends, bonds of solidarity. I like the people here and share meaning with them. However, if the order regresses and we begin clamping down on what we can do or where we can live, I will leave. But we are not doing that. The administration pretty much leaves us alone and lets us direct our own lives. But if I get my budget cut or am told I have to live with five to six other people, I will leave. Right now, there's no reason to leave, no pushes or pulls so why should I? I am happy where I am and with what I am doing so why rock the boat?"

All the women I interviewed expressed the fact that they value being part of a group that shares a commitment to social justice and spiritual values and provides feelings of solidarity and community for members. Most of these women said they had made a definite choice not to marry and have children and that being part of a religious community was more appealing than being a single person outside the order.

As another woman expressed it, "For me, it's a matter of convenience. It gives me a freedom, a base of operations, an identity, friendship with certain other women who make up *the* congregation for me. If they were not here, I would leave. They keep me plugged in. I never wanted to marry and have children so why leave now? There is not a good reason not to be here."

Interestingly, however, each woman articulated circumstances that would propel her to reconsider and probably leave. Rather than a total, unconditional commitment to the group, each one articulated the point at which the costs of staying would be too high. For several, this "line in the sand" was financial. If the order began to clamp down severely on personal budgets or the kind of life-style nuns can live, then these women said the price of staying would outweigh the rewards of financial independence outside the order. For several others, the line they drew was career related. As long as the order supports their careers and the work they do, they see value in belonging. These women are involved in work that benefits from their status as nun, particularly diocesan and parish work within the Catholic Church. As one woman put it, "The congregation gives me a credibility that I like in the work I do. My work is Church based and being a sister is an asset. We have single men and women also involved but being a sister gives me a credibility that I like. That connection with the Church helps me do what I want to do." However, if the order interfered with or hindered their careers, they would no longer see value in staying.

For several others, the turning point related to a reversal in the renewal and modernization process in the order. If the order begins to revert to authoritarianism or centralization of decision making, then they said they would be gone immediately.

Another issue of concern to these women was the stability of their friendship groups in the order. In addition to feeling part of the larger order, each one was obviously part of a smaller friendship group, a primary group that serves as a link between the individual and the order. If a substantial number of their friends leave, then it would not be the same order for these women, and they would have to seriously reconsider their own commitment. In fact, at an age-segregated meeting of those members under fifty, a major question they asked of each other was whether anyone was leaving and, if so, to make it public because it would affect the decisions of others in the peer group.

The fact that members, especially the productive, middle-aged members, are placing conditions on their commitment has ramifications for the administration of the order. Each decision is circumscribed by trying to anticipate the consequences of the action on various segments of the order. The alienation of this productive cohort would have serious organizational consequences, not only financial but also emotional and social.

In addition to asking why the middle-aged, productive cohort members are staying with an institution they admit is in demise, I interviewed six of the women who most recently entered the order. I asked them why they chose to enter an order with a high median age and one that might not survive over the course of their lifetimes. These new members were aware of the problems of the order, but they did not seem concerned about the future. Rather, they exhibited an excitement about being part of a group with which they shared spiritual values and the desire to do good in the world. As one young woman put it, "Whenever we gather together I identify with something that doesn't get nurtured out there. I identify with wanting the people of the world to know God is a Provident God. How I do it is different from others in the congregation but they want it too." She went on to say that during high school and college she was different from the other girls. While she dated and socialized, she was never satisfied with her life. She always wanted ideals that she was not reaching. When she met the Sisters of Service, "we clicked. I felt I had met some people who wanted what I wanted. I feel very at home in this order."

Another young nun also expressed feeling "at home" in the order. She valued being able to talk about God openly without feeling like an oddball or religious fanatic, which was often her experience in college. For her, and for all the new recruits I interviewed, the primary reason for entering the order and staying is having a strong group that shares the same values.

Although the youngest members of the order had many criticisms of the formation program, especially the tendency to treat recruits like children and adolescents rather than grown women, they were very positive toward the order and seemed fearless about its future. In fact, their attitudes toward the order were those of gratitude; they viewed the order almost as a savior. For many of them, the order is a haven, from both troubled families and peer groups that are antithetical to their values.

In summary, a major contributing factor to the organizational decline that religious orders are currently experiencing is the result of shifts occurring in the recruitment and socialization of new members. Like many other issues facing religious orders, recruitment and formation present an organizational dilemma for religious orders. The ideological and structural changes effected by Vatican II are based on a psychology that promotes religious life as a voluntary, deliberate choice on the part of mature women, rather than the kind of coercive persuasion that was often involved in the previous system in which young teenage girls, still in their early formative years, were attracted to religious life and socialized in a cloistered environment. Increasing the age requirement for recruits targeted older women with more experience; however, it affected both the potential pool of recruits as well as the type of socialization program conducive to training older women. As a result, fewer women requested entrance into the order.

Simultaneously, the way recruits were socialized shifted from a cloistered, regimented process to a more individualized, open program. Both the decreased numbers being socialized at any one time and the lack of regimentation diluted the peer group influence and the ability to inculcate group norms. In addition, as evident in chapter 6, the order itself is experiencing group anomie in terms of its mission. As a result, exactly what the recruit is being socialized into is less clear than in the former highly centralized, hierarchical system in which goals and mission were clearly specified.

Most members in the case study order have accepted the decline in new members as something permanent. There is little optimism that the order has a future in terms of membership replacements. However, the new associate membership program provides hope for many people. The rapid growth of the program and the apparent enthusiasm of these members have raised the hopes that the charism and spirit of the order will continue through the associate members and that somehow the associates will find ways to carry the order into a new century.

CHAPTER 8

Finances and the Vow of Poverty

In addition to changes in the authority structure in religious orders, major changes also occurred in the ways in which nuns relate to material goods and finances. While the vow of poverty has been central to religious profession since the beginning of religious orders, the meaning of the vow and the way it is lived out have shifted dramatically since Vatican II. In fact, while the system of authority was the primary vehicle of social control in religious orders prior to Vatican II, I contend that money matters are currently the major control mechanism. It is also the case that issues of authority and celibacy were primary reasons for the defections of nuns in the years immediately after the Council, but today issues of finances have become paramount in decisions to leave religious life (Ebaugh, 1984).

The organizational decline literature predicts that, under conditions of decline, organizations tend to reallocate resources with greater outlays going into internal affairs and less emphasis upon new markets and risky ventures. In an effort to halt decline and save the organization, increased attention is given to self-study and survival. In the case of religious orders, resources were not clearly reallocated; rather, orders increased both their internal and external foci. Self-studies and the creation of more internal administrative positions grew during the years of renewal; however, so did the allocation of resources toward new and riskier ministries. In this chapter I trace the twenty-five-year history of changes in both the vow of poverty and its institutionalization in the financial structure of the Sisters of Service.

Poverty and Financial Structure: 1965

As in the case of authority, it is impossible to understand the behavioral and structural implications of the vow of poverty without grasping the major shifts in defining the meaning and purpose of that vow in the life of a nun. Poverty was part of the overall Christian myth within which religious women vowed to live a life renouncing material goods.

Meaning of Poverty in the Traditional System

In pre–Vatican II religious life, poverty was viewed as divesting oneself of all riches and all attachments to material goods in order to be free to focus upon God and spiritual affairs. As early as the theology of Thomas Aquinas, matter was seen as not only separate from the spiritual realm but also on a lower plane than spiritual realities. The body and material goods were hindrances to the affairs of the soul and kept one from concentrating upon the higher realm of religious truths.

The rationale for poverty as a Christian virtue was based on that passage in the New Testament in which Jesus said, "It is easier for a camel to pass through the eye of a needle, than for the rich man to enter the kingdom of heaven." Likewise, Jesus said, "If a man does not renounce all he possesses, he cannot be My disciple." The purpose of the religious vow of poverty was the renunciation of material riches in order to take up the discipleship of Jesus to the fullest extent possible.

By the vow of poverty religious willingly gave up control over material goods. However, the spirit of the vow went far beyond material renunciation. Renunciation of pleasures derived from and made possible by material riches was the motivating spirit behind the vow. This included living as simply and austerely as possible and making oneself dependent on others for material survival.

While renunciation and austerity were one side of the coin of poverty, the purpose of a life of poverty was total trust in God's providence. Like children dependent on their parents or the birds of the air and the lilies of the field who did not have to toil for their living, dedicated religious were encouraged to depend for their survival on God. Dependence, therefore, was interpreted as a Christian virtue on the part of those who renounced material goods for the sake of the heavenly kingdom.

Structural Consequences of the Vow of Poverty

The Sisters of Service took a simple vow of poverty whereby they rejected control over and use of all material possessions. Although some orders of nuns professed solemn vows and thereby renounced ownership of all material goods, simple vows enabled the individual to maintain dowries and inheritance but forfeited the use of these goods during one's lifetime. In the event of leaving the order, the nun was entitled to these possessions. Before taking vows, the nun made a will in which she specified the disposition of these assets upon her death. She had the legal freedom to name whomever or whatever as heirs, but it was customary to leave material possessions to the order. During a nun's lifetime, she could give the order the rights to invest the principal contained in inheritances and use the interest from such investments.

In return for renouncing all material possessions and vowing to live a simple, poor life, the order assured the individual that it would provide for her livelihood. The order managed such provision without the individual being aware of, or having to tend to, any financial transactions. Shelter was provided in terms of congregational- or parish-owned buildings; food was bought, prepared, and served by domestic nuns in the order or, occasionally, by hired lay help; medical needs were provided in the infirmary maintained by the order or, if necessary, by physicians well known to the order who usually treated the nuns without charge; personal articles such as soap, toothpaste, school supplies, as well as clothing were provided in a common storage area. Education was provided, by and large, at the university owned and run by the order.

As a result of this system, nuns conducted virtually no financial transactions and rarely handled money. Local communities usually had a "kitty," a box with a small amount of petty cash that nuns used in the rare event they needed bus fare for a trip to the doctor's office. This was carefully accounted for immediately upon one's return.

After completing the formation stage and making vows in the order, nuns were assigned to various jobs, usually within institutions owned and/or staffed by the order. On the whole, this meant parochial schools (grade schools and high schools), Catholic hospitals, and, in a few cases, social work agencies. Nuns were compensated with room and board, a meager stipend, and some form of transportation. In 1965 the average monthly stipend in parish-owned schools was about $150. The arrangement for employment was between the order and the pastor or other administrator. Nuns were seldom aware of the contractual arrangements or the remuneration. Any changes in such agreements were negotiated directly with the administration.

Financial affairs in the local community where nuns lived were handled by the local superior and a treasurer appointed by the superior. The individual nun had no involvement and usually no knowledge of either her earnings or her expenses. Therefore, neither remuneration nor costs were ever conceptualized or accounted for on the basis of individuals; rather, they were based on the needs of the local community.

Although the vow of poverty, strictly speaking, refers to the renunciation of the use of personal property, the spirit of the vow has far broader implications—namely, freedom from concern with material things in order to focus upon spiritual matters. Sins against the vow were defined as undue attention focused upon things not of the spirit, as well as a lack of trust in God's provident care.

The elaborate system of permissions was part of the spirit of poverty. By having to ask permission for the use of any and all material things, the individual experienced her poverty and dependence. Owning nothing, however, had the explicit purpose of freeing oneself from material worries in order to be totally able to give oneself to God and the spread of His kingdom on earth.

The financial affairs of the order were handled primarily by the treasurer general of the order, an individual elected by the general chapter. The role of the treasurer general was to administer financial decisions made by the superior general and her council.

As a nonprofit organization, the Sisters of Service are eligible for tax-exempt status. Therefore, it was not required to file the usual federal tax forms. In addition, the stipends that members received for their work in other church-related, tax-exempt organizations were also not subject to federal income tax. In addition, prior to 1973 the nuns were neither allowed to contribute to nor did they receive social security or welfare benefits; thereby federal reporting forms were streamlined.

Both health care and retirement needs were taken care of by the order. Given the fact that the order was at its numerical height with 734 members and a median age in the low forties, both the retirement and health needs of members were minimal in relation to the number of employed members.

In summary, by renouncing the possession and use of material goods, the vow of poverty in traditional religious orders freed the individual from the cares and worries created in the struggle to survive materially in this world so that she could be totally devoted to the mission of spreading God's kingdom on earth. Such renunciation resulted in an attitude of childlike dependence on God's providence manifest through the order that promised to take care of all material needs.

The Transition Period: Communal Sharing

Two major emphases in the Vatican II Council documents provided the conceptual shifts that affected discussion and reevaluation of the vow of poverty and its structural implications in the decade immediately following the Council: (1) the insistence on greater responsibility and involvement on the part of individual nuns in the renewal process; and (2) identification with the poor.

Most religious orders, including the Sisters of Service, focused first on establishing greater individual responsibility as a hallmark of renewal. The period of the late 1960s and early 1970s was spent assuring that nuns became more aware of themselves as individuals benefiting from and contributing to a community. Essential to this thrust was the idea that a group of dedicated religious women working toward communal goals could achieve outcomes, such as witnessing to Christian living and missionizing in the world in ways that were more difficult, if not impossible, for married or single people. In addition, the value of community life became a major issue, in terms of both defining a mission for the order and assuring that mutual support and solidarity among members were rich experiences that met social and emotional needs of members.

This focus upon the community nature of religious life manifested itself in redefining the vow of poverty as the vow of "communal sharing." Because nuns realized that they did not live in poverty in the sense of material deprivation, there was a reluctance to profess a life of poverty. Unlike the truly poor in the world, nuns were assured of being provided with basic sustenance. Not only were basic material needs met by the order, but nuns also tended to live in middle-class dwellings, eat wholesome and plentiful food, have medical needs taken care of, have the opportunity for educational and professional development, and be able to enjoy leisure time activities such as television, concerts, good books, and periodic travel. Compared to the growing numbers of truly disadvantaged in American society, nuns were quite well off.

Rather than emphasize material poverty, during the 1970s the Sisters of Service focused upon the characteristic of their material life-styles that did distinguish them from most of society, namely, the communal aspect of their material goods. By renouncing the use of personal property and contributing all earned income to the community, the individual nun was dependent upon the largess of communal sharing.

Although the communal aspect of religious life did not change after Vatican II, attitudes shifted regarding the dependence of the individual upon the community. Previously dependence itself was defined as religious submission and denial of self for a holy cause, but during the transition years the notion of dependency was replaced with the idea of voluntarily choosing to contribute material goods to the common cause so that a corporate mission could be sustained. Individuals, now active participants in managing material goods, were given a sense of personal responsibility for the well-being of the community.

Structural Changes

A number of changes made in the order's financial system during the transition years grew out of and incorporated the redefined vow of poverty. In the spirit of communal sharing and financial planning, in the early 1970s the order instigated a system of centralized financing in which stipends and salaries were sent directly to the central administration. Each local community then prepared an annual budget that had to be approved by the central administration. The treasurer of the order sent monthly checks in the approved amount to the local house for communal expenses, such as rent, food, household goods, and so on.

Unlike the former system, each nun was also given a predetermined amount for "personal needs," such as clothing, recreation, personal articles, or travel. This amount, varying over time, ranged from $25 per month in the early 1970s to $60 later in the decade. Until 1978 the amount was increased for individuals by special request. Each nun was required to keep an accounting of expenditures, which was submitted on an annual basis. At the end of each year, any unspent money was returned to the central administration.

Along with the initiation of budgets and individual allowances came discussion, lectures, reading material, and advice on the relationship of the use of money to one's vow of communal sharing. Central to this instruction was the insistence that the vow was a commitment to communal sharing of material goods, and this meant individual responsibility for the welfare of the group.

To help members be aware of communal needs, each summer during the general assembly the financial state of the order was reported in terms of assets, liabilities, income, expenditures, and projected needs of the order in coming years. By the mid 1970s, as median age in the order was rising and more and more nuns were retiring or approaching retirement age, the financial picture of the order was becoming less optimistic. It became obvious that serious planning was required to provide for the future retirement of members. Along with reports on projections, members were asked to be conservative in their budget requests in order to contribute to the overall needs of the order.

For decades in the order, finances were seen as the responsibility of the treasurer general, in collaboration with the superior general and her council. Nuns were totally excluded from the inner workings of the financial structure. During the 1970s that changed and finances became a topic of open discussion along with a sense of involvement and responsibility on the part of each member. In addition, outside advisers, such as accountants, CPAs, lawyers, and investment brokers, were brought in for advice on financial planning for the order. In many ways, during the decade of the 1970s the Sisters of Service moved from an isolated total institution, autocratically run, to a corporate voluntary organization in which members join together to achieve communal goals and act responsibly for the well-being and future of the group. This shift in organizational form accompanied a major shift in the way in which members defined their vow of poverty, away from emphasis upon self-denial and renunciation toward a focus upon communal sharing for the sake of corporate goals.

The Vow of Poverty: 1990

During the 1989 and 1990 general assemblies of the Sisters of Service the three major issues that consumed much of the agenda related to the vow of poverty: (1) emphasis upon the Church's mission to "stand with the materially poor"; (2) what it means to live a simple life-style; and (3) concerns regarding the financial status of the order.

The Vow of Poverty as Standing with the Materially Poor

The most dramatic change in discussions of poverty during these assemblies was the prominent role given to considerations of what it means to identify with the poor in the world. While the notion of identifying with the materially poor was put forward by Vatican II as a central Christian stance, it took almost fifteen years before many religious orders, including the Sisters of Service, took the principle seriously as a basis for living out the vow of poverty. Only when individual responsibility and the Christian value of communal living became well understood and accepted as a norm did nuns begin to relate their vow of poverty to the larger issue of the materially poor in the world.

To understand what the new stance means for orders, it is important to understand how the Council defined the mission of the Church as one of "solidarity with the materially poor." In his announcement of the Council, Pope John XXIII called for an updating of the Church in keeping with the signs of the times, including the alarming numbers of poor and oppressed peoples in the world. In a previous encyclical, *Mater et Magistra* (1961), he noted that the Church in Latin America was too closely linked with oppressive political and economic regimes that hindered the human rights of the poor. Pope John claimed that peace, poverty, and human rights should be the central concerns of committed Christians.

The Council delegates recognized that the gospel of Christianity, institutionalized over the centuries into health, education, and welfare services, had become deeply entangled with political, economic, and social institutions that frequently disadvantaged the poor rather than bettering their condition (Neal, 1990). As a result, the Council admitted that a general restructuring was needed to free the Church and its social involvements from unjust customs and exploitation. The Church focused attention on eliminating the causes of poverty rather than, as was true previously, on alleviating its results. The Church moved from close support of established systems to a basic challenge to those same systems.

In grappling with the meaning of a vow of poverty in the post–Vatican II era, the Sisters of Service order faces many issues that are being discussed by religious women across the United States (see Schneiders, 1986). Many of these issues relate to the increased awareness of global interdependence in the world today. No matter how simple a life-style nuns adopt, they realize that it is luxurious compared to that of many people in both the United States and third world countries. Furthermore, in itself material poverty is seen as an evil that both political systems as well as the Church want to eradicate, not imitate. Therefore, "opting for the materially poor" does not mean living as the poor do in terms of destitution and want but rather working for the rights and betterment of disadvantaged peoples.

A second point of discussion focuses upon the fact that individual and community acts of sharing and hospitality seem almost pointless in the face of the millions who suffer homelessness, starvation, and social deprivations. The problems of the poor are too immense to be addressed by individual acts of mercy. In addition, voluntary renunciation of luxuries or unnecessary goods and services does nothing to redistribute material goods.

Third, poverty is seen not as a condition willingly chosen by those who live in it, nor as the result of selfish choices but, rather, as a systemic evil that results from policies and politics of specific institutions and governments and must be dealt with institutionally.

Long and intense discussions in the order establishing the above principles have resulted in a societal and corporate focus for living out the vow of poverty. Attention is now upon individual and organizational actions that can have an impact on the institutions that are perpetuating poverty for a large number of the earth's people.

The theme for the 1990 general assembly of the Sisters of Service was entitled "Global Awareness," and the keynote address was given by Dr. Patricia Mische, a laywoman who cofounded Global Education Associates. She argued that the contemporary focus of the vow of poverty for religious must include a commitment to bettering the environment for all people but especially for the poor around the world who often feel the detrimental effects of environmental pollution more directly than the better-off in societies. To solve environmental problems, concerned citizens as well as groups must focus upon creating policy changes within those institutions in the world that are most directly involved with polluting the earth. Although individual actions to protect the environment can make a difference when enough people are committed to them, radical changes must occur at the national policy level and within large corporations. She appealed to the order to take public stances against laws and practices that further global pollution and to collectively promote policies and programs aimed at responsible control. Throughout the assembly meetings, the theme of global awareness and action motivated many discussions and decisions.

Several years prior to the assembly, the general council in the order approved the purchase of stock in Chevron Oil Company with the explicit intent of filing stockholder's resolutions regarding the pollution of air, soil, and water in the vicinity of a uranium-processing facility. In addition, the order bought stock in a power and light company in order to have a voice in a nuclear project being considered. The order also took a stand not to invest in the top one hundred defense contractors who are heavily involved in the nuclear arms buildup. From these examples it is evident that the meaning of the vow of poverty in the order has shifted greatly in the years since Vatican II.

Early in the decade of the 1980s the order also established a social justice office within the community and released one of its members from a wage-earning position to serve as full-time director. The primary goal of the office was to educate members in the order about issues of social justice as well as developing programs and policies whereby the order would be more involved in issues of social justice. Several years after it was established, the office became part of an intercommunity social justice program staffed and supported by a number of religious orders in the local area.

In each monthly newsletter published by and for members in the order, the social justice staff person has a column in which she educates the members about issues of social justice at both national and local levels. She describes very explicitly actions that both the order and individual nuns can take to effect these issues. Names, addresses, and telephone numbers of public officials involved in these issues are listed, and she encourages members to contact these officials and push for legislation that promotes social justice, especially for the disadvantaged. During election campaigns, officials who have taken public stances against social justice legislation are singled out, as well as those who have a record of supporting legislation that benefits the poor.

Just prior to the 1990 general assembly, leadership in the order also encouraged nuns to attend a public forum of candidates running for local office. Transportation was provided for everyone who wanted to go, including the retired nuns. More than a hundred nuns in the order showed up at the political gathering. Many of them were vocal in asking questions and challenging the candidates regarding their stands on social issues.

During the late 1970s and throughout the 1980s, motivated by a growing awareness of needs of the poor and disadvantaged, the order allowed a number of its members to take jobs working with poverty programs and in public-sector jobs that focused upon the poor. For more than ten years, two members have worked in a political action group that organizes local communities to effect political action on their behalf. The order now has nuns working with the poor in Appalachia, on an Indian reservation, with disadvantaged blacks in various areas of the South, in a legal aid agency, and in various programs for Hispanics in the Southwest. Although some of these jobs are well salaried, many nuns in these positions are drawing very little remuneration.

An issue on the agenda for the order during the early 1990s is that of providing sanctuary for needy refugees. The order has not yet taken a public stance on the sanctuary movement; however, some members of the order want to use some congregational buildings to shelter refugees. The decision has many legal and political ramifications, as well as the potential to draw disapproval from Church authorities. However, some among the members argue that providing sanctuary is a responsibility for groups that publicly profess concern for the needy of the world, especially for religious who profess a vow of poverty.

Discussion of poverty in terms of corporate responsibility to identify with and aid the poor of the world in every way possible is a far cry from the pre–Vatican II interpretation of the vow of poverty as a means of renouncing self in order to be filled with His graces and gifts. In the words of sociologist Max Weber, the vow of poverty has shifted from an "other-worldly" to a "this-worldly" orientation.

The Vow of Poverty as Living a Simple Life-Style

A second aspect of identifying with the materially poor—one gaining increased attention in religious orders, including the Sisters of Service—is a reevaluation of the life-styles lived by nuns. Now that many nuns have cars at their disposal, modern equipment in their homes and offices, access to mass media, personal budgets, the freedom to wear contemporary dress and accept gifts from family and friends, and the ability to make purchases without asking permission, the life-style of most nuns is much more affluent and comfortable than in the traditional system. However, as the Sisters of Service become more and more conscious of the poor in society and take a corporate stance to identify with and assist the poor, questions regarding the sisters' own life-styles are being raised. How is it possible to identify with the poor and gain their trust if nuns live a style of life significantly better than that of the poor? Is it right to enjoy a materially advantaged position in society and, at the same time, profess a vow of poverty when so many people in the world do not take a vow of poverty but are forced to live more materially poor than the vowed poor? Have nuns been lured into the consumerism of society rather than challenging those preoccupations that might replace spiritual strivings?

One of the first, and most controversial, ways in which the discussion of life-style arose in the order was in relation to dress. Although the Sisters of Service have not been wearing a uniform religious habit for twenty years, the formal norms specify that dress must be modest and simple. In addition, jewelry should be limited to the congregational ring, which was given when the nun made her vows, and a simple cross pin. By the 1990 assembly meeting, some nuns were wearing brightly colored dresses, pant suits, and jeans, as well as jewelry and makeup. Several times during the meeting the issue of whether such attire is appropriate for nuns was raised, especially in the context of whether it constitutes "simple attire." Several nuns responded publicly during "open mike" time; they justified their attire on the basis of personal choice and argued that the order has no right to legislate such an individual matter. The argument was also made that different occupational settings demand different appropriate attire. In particular, several nuns who work as professionals in public institutions argued that it was necessary for them to dress well and to wear jewelry and makeup in order to gain the respect of their non-Catholic colleagues.

The discussion, which provoked a lot of emotion and disagreement among members, lead to two outcomes in the order: (1) further discussion of the relationship between simple life-style and the vow of poverty, and (2) a distinction between public and private issues among the members.

The issue of simple life-style has not yet been resolved in the order even though the new constitution states it as an explicit goal: "Though our own conditions of material poverty vary, the virtue of poverty demands that we live simply, maintaining only what we need to carry out our mission." The financial problems that the order is currently facing in terms of retirement needs of the members is causing the simple life-style question to be framed in the context of belt tightening to remedy the bleak financial picture.

The public-versus-private question raised at the 1989 assembly lead to a video, which the administration prepared, in which "experts" from various areas (sociology, law, theology, public policy) addressed the question of what is public and what is private in group life. The video was shown and discussed at various local meetings of the members during the 1989–1990 academic year. No distinct policy changes resulted from the discussions, but they provided a common framework for dialogue on these issues and a public forum in which the issues could be discussed objectively.

Financial Status of the Order

The third major concern at the 1989 and 1990 general assemblies was the current financial state of the order in the light of projected financial needs for the future. In 1990 the median age of members reached seventy. Almost 33 percent of the membership was retired. To complicate matters even more, 50 percent of current earners are older than sixty, which means that most of them, too, will be retiring in the next ten to fifteen years. The primary financial problem facing the order is the current and future cost of retirement for its members.

The reason for the retirement problem today stems from the system of service that characterized religious orders as they began staffing parish schools in the early history of this country. Because most immigrant parishes were poor, the nuns were poorly compensated for their services, often remunerated with nothing but room and board; it was the rare case in which the parish could provide a monetary stipend as well. Health needs were taken care of by parishioners in medical and dental practice or sympathetic doctors and dentists who treated the nuns free of charge. Parishioner mechanics, carpenters, electricians, and plumbers took care of the nuns' material needs. Virtually all the nuns' needs were taken care of with "in kind" rather than monetary payments. The provision of benefits, such as health insurance and retirement, was nonexistent.

The acquisition of liquid assets (i.e., cash) was minuscule until the 1950s and 1960s, when parishes began contributing small stipends to the support of the nuns. These usually amounted to $100 to $150 per month for each nun.

With the large numbers of new recruits, all in their teenage years, entering during the middle decades of this century, for a long time the cost of retirement was not felt in orders. In the 1960s the Conference of Major Superiors of Women was beginning to question the inadequacies of nuns' salaries; at that time not only were proportionately few nuns of retirement age, but also the large pool of earners was sufficient to take care of those not earning. The financial burden of retirement was, therefore, not yet being experienced in most orders.

As a result of these factors, the Sisters of Service, as is true of most orders in the United States, had not invested in any retirement program, including social security. Only in 1973 were tax-exempt institutions given the option to participate in social security. The Sisters of Service, by choosing this option, thereby qualified for benefits. Currently, the order pays about $100,000 in social security taxes each year and receives about $850,000 in benefits.

In 1967 the order began to project future retirement needs by setting aside monies for a retirement program. In the past several years, financial advisers hired by the order have projected the amount necessary over the next several decades to support retired members, and the order began a serious investment program to try to amass the capital to fund the recommended program; however, to achieve the projected goal the principal must be invested, and the interest from the principal must be reinvested each year. Although the order was able to raise much of the principal by means of selling some property and investing wisely, currently its operating expenses far exceed the income generated by earners. It is, therefore, using most of the interest from the retirement principal to provide ongoing operating money for the retirement center.

About three years ago the retirement problem for Catholic nuns, and priests as well, became so acute that religious orders of men and women formed a national coalition, in collaboration with the National Bishops Conference, with two goals in mind: (1) to solicit retirement funds from Catholic parishes, and (2) to establish criteria for higher compensation for workers in Church settings. The coalition, called the Tri-Conference Retirement Project, has established a fund-raising drive in every Catholic diocese in the United States. The drive is framed in terms of justice: members remind parishioners of the decades of service that priests and nuns have provided to Catholic parishes with little or no monetary compensation, a history resulting in the dire financial situation in which religious orders find themselves today. The campaign, having raised $25 million in 1988, is one of the most successful ever run in Catholic dioceses. The Tri-Conference has simultaneously set up a team to evaluate the needs of each religious order and has allocated campaign funds on the basis of need. The Sisters of Service received approximately $150,000 from the Tri-Conference in 1989.

In October 1984, the Sisters of Service, aware of the precarious state of their financial future owing to the increasing median age of members and retirement projections, hired the firm of Arthur Andersen and Company to conduct an actuarial study and make financial recommendations to the order. Representatives of the company presented a summary of their findings to the 1985 general assembly. While most recommendations were aimed at policy changes at the corporate level (discussed in the following section), two outcomes of the report generated a lot of attention among members and set the agendas for the next four or five assemblies. First, members became more aware of the financial situation in the order and requested more information and education regarding finances. Second, the report and its ramifications reminded members that they are part of a corporate reality and that each member has a responsibility for the good of the whole. With the public presentation of the Andersen report, the old notion that finances are the responsibility of the central administration was laid to final rest, and finances suddenly became a public issue. At the request of members, the administration established an ongoing educational program on finances. This includes reports and discussion at the local level, a video presentation, announcements and updating of financial decisions in the in-house newsletter, annual financial reports at the general assemblies, and, most recently, a periodic financial report sent to each member with her monthly check for personal expenses.

The Sisters of Service order over the past twenty-five years has moved through three stages in its involvement of members in the financial affairs of the order. Traditionally, members were uninvolved and uninformed in regard to financial matters, which, after all, were of "this world" and could easily distract one from focus upon spiritual concerns. During the transition years of renewal (the 1970s and early 1980s) focus was upon individual responsibility and maturity in matters financial; nuns learned to handle money in terms of salaries and budgets. By 1990 the financial emphasis had shifted to a focus upon corporate planning and responsibility for the future of the group.

Current Financial Structure of the Order

The Sisters of Service uses centralized financing whereby all earners send their salaries directly to the central administration. If possible, checks are made out directly to the order; if not, the individual nun endorses her check to the order. To maintain tax-exempt status, whenever possible, work contracts are made between the employer and the order rather than with individual members.

On the basis of a recommendation from Arthur Andersen, the central administration calculated an average of what it takes each year to support each member in the order. Even though that figure was $26,000, the administration decided to set $21,600 as the minimum stipend that a member could accept as a condition for employment. Of this, $12,000 must be in monetary terms, $1,200 in retirement benefits, $1,200 for medical insurance, $2,400 for auto expenses, and $400 per month for housing. Each member, therefore, who makes a minimum of $21,600 is carrying her load in terms of cost of living. If a member wants to accept a job with a salary below the specified minimum, she is required to request a "subsidy" from the central administration. Currently, ninety-nine members (37.2 percent) under age sixty-four (defined as "earners") are subsidized by the order for various reasons, while 30.3 percent of the members receive full compensation. Subsidized ministries include jobs of members who work in institutions and agencies incapable of paying the established salary; many of these latter are low income and/or parish settings. Given the order's commitment to serving the materially poor, requests for subsidies in these instances are usually approved. The corporate mission of the order has tended to override financial concerns.

Although a substantial number of members are working in subsidized jobs, simultaneously the central administration is encouraging those nuns who are able to take jobs with high salaries to do so in order to support those members in subsidized jobs. At the 1990 general assembly a topic of discussion was how many low paying, subsidized jobs the order could afford and under what conditions such jobs should be approved. Some nuns question the large number of members who are being subsidized and are requesting a policy indicating the criteria for subsidies.

The ability of the order to subsidize salaries is one issue being raised by the financial difficulties of the order. Simultaneously, the topic of personal budgets is another, very sensitive, issue. Each member, regardless of occupation or earning capacity, submits an annual personal budget request. These requests vary substantially, depending on the living situation of the member. Currently, ninety-four nuns are living alone or with nuns in other orders, compared with seven prior to 1967 and about thirty in 1967. Most of those living singly in earlier years were nuns away studying at educational institutions. Today nuns are choosing to live alone for a variety of reasons, including diversified work settings and personal space for psychological growth. The increase in single dwellings, however, is having an impact on the financial picture because it normally is more expensive to live alone than in a group, where housing expenses, food, and general maintenance costs are shared.

Budget requests also vary depending on the type of jobs of members. Some nuns in high paying, professional, non-Church settings argue that they have financial requirements of dress, continuing education, entertainment, and work expenses necessary to maintain their jobs. They expressed some resentment that they generate a disproportionate amount of income and yet their budgets are judged on the same basis as the less financially productive members.

The above concerns are indicative of the fact that religious orders are gradually drifting from a form of organization based on covenental social relations to one in which contractual relations predominate (Bromley and Busching, 1988). Contractual social relations involve a logic of calculative involvement and individual interest while covenental relations are based on a logic of moral involvement and unity. Religious orders were founded as covenental groups dedicated to altruistic communal goals, but the modernization of the past several decades has involved more and more contractual negotiations.

During the time of the Second Vatican Council and immediately thereafter, when the exodus of nuns from their orders was at its height, many ex-nuns articulated the requirements of celibacy and obedience as major reasons for leaving (Ebaugh, 1977; San Giovanni, 1978). However, in the past decade financial concerns have replaced the earlier reasons (Ebaugh, 1984). In these instances, the issue of financial insecurity of the order is not, however, the important consideration. Rather, nuns are opting to leave because of the financial constraints they feel they suffer in their orders. During interviews with members in the Sisters of Service, the major complaint voiced by younger members in the order was the social control they feel being exercised through control of personal budgets. Many of these younger nuns, especially those in high paying jobs, said that they might leave the order because of the personal restrictions they feel being exercised in terms of their budgets. These concerns were usually expressed in terms of lack of trust on the part of the central administration. As one younger nun expressed it, "They trust me to hold down a $40,000 a year job but not to have the good sense to know what my financial needs are." Another member said, "If I ever leave, it will be because I am treated like a child when it comes to money matters."

While many nuns in the order were protesting the practice of budget approvals, the central administration was struggling to engage in rational financial planning for the future of the order. To do this, it was necessary to project a corporate budget and determine both income and expenses on a yearly basis. Without some control over expenses, the administration had no way of projecting cash flow and engaging in "belt tightening" to meet operating expenses, especially the spiraling retirement costs. By the summer of 1990 the issue of money had become a sensitive subject in the order. The administration felt the need to inform members of the financial condition of the order, and yet, in the process, some members resented the control over their personal lives that such financial disclosure and planning indicated.

The Sisters of Service is no longer a small group of women dedicated to Christian service, as their founder envisioned, but over the years, with the pressures of bureaucratization and federal requirements, it has become a large corporation with an operating budget of $5 million a year. As a legal entity, the order enters into various legal contracts, invests its monies in the stock and bond markets, is liable for certain taxes, deals with medicare and social security programs, and must comply with various federal and state requirements for nonprofit corporations.

Because of its complexity as a corporate body, the order has recently hired financial experts to assist in financial matters. Two paid money managers select investments vehicles; several stock brokers are hired to buy and sell stocks and bonds; three laymen sit on an Investment Advisers Committee, along with four nuns to review investments and set investment policies.

In November 1988, the order was advised by its financial and legal advisers to change its charter from a member corporation to a memberless one in order to be protected against liability suits filed against individual members of the order. With the consent of the membership, this action was taken and the formal name of the order changed from Congregation of the Sisters of Service to Congregation of Service, Inc.

Dilemmas Created by the New System

The redefinition of the vow of poverty, along with the attitudes and structures that have evolved in the order within the past decade, has created a number of organizational dilemmas. By definition a dilemma is a choice between equally undesirable alternatives. Given the more open structures and emphasis upon greater individuality in post–Vatican II orders, a redefinition of the vow of poverty was almost inevitable. Although the notion of renunciation and austerity in the old system dovetailed with a vow of obedience that stressed dependency and compliance, these views were disjunctive in the renewed order. It was necessary, therefore, to reevaluate the vow of poverty and its relevance in the new structures of religious life. The new ideas, however, of individual budgets, better life-styles, nonuniform dress, and greater individual choice in careers and job placement made it more difficult to control the financial life of the order.

In addition, as the corporate nature of the order became more complex and members began to view the order as a corporate entity as well as a communal association of dedicated women, altruistic commitments to the group were more difficult to sustain. The situation that developed in the Sisters of Service parallels closely the evolution that occurred in the numerous U.S. communes, developing in the nineteenth century and reemerging in the late 1960s and early 1970s. Interestingly, the decline and breakup of the Oneida community is traced by Carden (1969) to the time when John Humphrey Noyes, the founder, turned from his earlier insistence on group autonomy to an emphasis upon continuous self-realization of the individual. "Ironically," Carden says, "it was probably not the community's inconsistent attitude toward its own religious principles but its consistently strong emphasis on education which allowed children to follow a somewhat different course from that taken by their parents." All children were encouraged to read widely so they grew up with an appreciation of literary scholarship, with scientific training, and with at least a vicarious taste for the attractions of the outside world. In time, the younger members in the community were allowed to take jobs outside the commune and to receive compensation on the basis of their individual talents and skills. This led to inequalities in life-styles, unequal monetary contributions to the community funds, and eventual comparisons and bickering over the way material resources were allocated to members. As Oneida shifted from its original toy-making industry to the more lucrative manufacturing of Oneida silver, it became necessary to restructure as a corporation. This shift and its repercussions are reflected in the title of Carden's story of the community: *Oneida: Utopian Community to Modern Corporation.*

Gillian Lindt Gollin (1967) traces a similar demise process in a Moravian community. As the commune grew in size and complexity, members were allowed greater freedom in the choice of jobs and life-styles. Gradually, the altruistic goals of the commune were lost as members became involved in their own interests and self-pursuits.

The literature on communes shows quite clearly that disagreements over financial matters are frequently the cause, or at least the precipitating factor, in the breakup of the group (see Zablocki, 1980). As long as commune members contribute equally to the material well-being of the group, both giving and receiving according to ability and need, survival is possible. But when members begin to earn money individually and work on the basis of individual contracts rather than group commitments, altruism tends to disintegrate, and invidious comparisons among members become common.

In traditional religious orders finances were not a public issue. Contracts were made between the order and employers; remunerations were collected by the order. Members were expected to cooperate with whatever job assignments they were given and had little, if any, input into their placements. In return, the needs of members were taken care of by the order.

With the renewal and adaptation agenda set by Vatican II, it was virtually impossible to maintain these attitudes of secrecy and dependency. As nuns became more involved with the renewal process and more attuned to ideas of maturity and self-development, it was inevitable that the interpretation of the vow of poverty would change and that the old structures that promoted dependency would be supplanted. Although the new emphasis upon individuality and self-actualization has resulted in less dependence and greater self-determination, the organizational implications of the shift are evident in the problems the order faces today. Questioning of personal budgets and life-styles by the central administration is interpreted by some members as distrust; inequities between what is earned and what is allowed for personal use are being accentuated; questions of why some members are being subsidized are being raised; great diversity in life-style is occurring; and, finally, issues of meaning are surfacing as members begin to wonder what is unique about religious life in the modern world.

The order had little choice: it was propelled into the new ways of thinking by both the Council and the culture of mid-twentieth-century America. Therein lies the dilemma. The order, likewise, has little choice in solving the dilemma. From an organizational standpoint the most obvious solution to these problems is to recreate a sense of community by becoming committed as an entity to some specific works such as missionary activity in a third world country, servicing the needs of an immigrant or poor community in the United States, or reviving an educational system in a designated diocese. Contracts would again be made with the order as an entity, and monetary matters would be communal in nature. This scenario is theoretically possible, but practically it is unrealistic primarily because of the commitments and attitudes of the members who are unwilling to give up individual careers and freedoms. For many members, survival of the order is no longer a major concern. More important is the sense that one's own meaningful work contributes to the Church and the modern world. As long as membership in the order promotes and sustains this goal, people stay. If, however, the order jeopardizes or challenges what individuals value, then some members are prepared either to leave the order or simply to refuse to comply. Presently, the order has virtually no mechanisms of social control over members, other than in the area of budget requests. Because the order depends upon the salaries of these members, the risk of alienating and losing members, especially those drawing high salaries, is too risky. For these reasons, the demise of the order in time seems almost inevitable.

In summary, let me return to the prediction that declining organizations to assure their survival tend to reallocate resources internally. Although the Sisters of Service has commissioned several self-studies, including the financial review by Arthur Andersen, and have established several new internal offices, such as a development office for fund raising and a ministries office to assist members in job placement, the order continues to commit resources to nonlucrative ventures. Relatively few members are working in professional settings where they draw competitive salaries. Most employed members are in jobs subsidized by the order in terms of adequate salary. The administration has placed the service value of these jobs above financial considerations, even though the order is engaged in deficit spending. Such action indicates that commitment to values and service is more important to the order than organizational survival.

CHAPTER 9

Nuns as Feminists

In her review of the book, *The Courage to Choose: An American Nun's Story* (Griffin, 1975) Betty Friedan says that one of the most dramatic chapters of the entire modern women's movement is the emergence of the American nun from the cloister to define and assert her personhood in society (Friedan, 1975). Friedan recognized the tremendous revolution that took place in the late 1960s and throughout the 1970s as American nuns adapted to contemporary social conditions by radically altering convent life-styles. These changes were frequently made against vehement objections by a male-dominated Church hierarchy.

However, the impact of American nuns upon the feminist movement in the United States is much broader and more direct than the example that they set as self-directed women in a male Church. For decades prior to the renewal of Vatican II, nuns unwittingly set an example for the Catholic girls they taught as educated, career women, and they provided career options for such girls. In the early years of renewal, immediately after the Council, the expression of feminism among American nuns took the form of organizational confrontation with Roman authorities on the part of several religious orders. During the decade of the 1980s and into the 1990s, religious women are openly identifying with the Women's Movement and articulating their role as feminists as part of their mission in a male-dominated Church. In this chapter, I describe the part that American nuns have played in the history of feminism in this country.

Traditional Nuns as Unwitting Feminists

Until the last twenty-five years, the feminist role of Catholic nuns was basically unwitting and unanticipated (Ebaugh 1978). In fact, prior to the Women's Movement of the 1960s, the stereotype of the Catholic nun was one of an obedient, meek, humble servant of the male-dominated Church. As Friedan accurately states, nuns were the "feminine mystique at its most extreme." However, despite stereotypes and the outward demeanor of nuns, in three ways Catholic nuns were unwitting feminists: as role models for Catholic girls in immigrant communities, as professional women in various career settings, and as single women in a society where the wife-mother role was normative.

Nuns as Role Models

For immigrant Catholic girls who were taught by nuns in Catholic parochial schools, the model of the educated career woman portrayed by nuns was the only alternative to the wife-mother role they saw in their communities. The history of the Catholic Church in the United States is the history of Catholic immigrant groups that came from various parts of Europe and settled in urban and rural areas and small towns in this country. These settlements were either located around an already established ethnic church or one that was soon constructed by the immigrants. After establishing a local church, the next step was to erect a parochial school in which children were taught by Catholic nuns, usually brought over from the local group's community of origin. Until recently, the Catholic Church strongly recommended that Catholic children be educated in parochial schools. Most Catholic children, therefore, attended Catholic grammar as well as high schools. Nuns usually administered and constituted the main faculty in these schools.

For the Catholic girls in these parochial schools, nuns were role models of women who had opted for lives of dedication and service to causes above and beyond individual families. They were seen as courageous women of character who sacrificed personal needs and desires in the service of other people. In addition, the mysterious life of the convent, the intrigue of unusual garb, and the esteem in which the Catholic community held these women aroused not only the curiosity but also the idealism of many Catholic girls.

Immigrant Catholic families have traditionally been large. The necessity of caring for many children, plus cultural norms that stipulated a traditional feminine role for women meant that young girls could look forward to a life of hard work in what would probably be a working-class home. For those who dreamed of escaping the traditional responsibilities of marriage and family, the path of the convent often appeared to be the only alternative open to them. In that era careers for women were not readily available for any social class, ethnic, or religious group. The only exception was the "old maid school teacher," looked upon negatively in most of these immigrant communities. Unlike "spinsters," nuns had high status in Catholic circles. It was considered a blessing from God to have a daughter "chosen" to enter the convent.

Simultaneously, in the first half of the twentieth century it was difficult for Catholic girls to receive college educations. Many of them came from working-class families where education was a financial hardship and considered appropriate only for privileged males in the family who could use higher education as an avenue of social mobility. For girls who valued higher education, entering a convent was an ideal, and often sole, route because a nun's educational expenses were taken care of by the order.

The fact that education was a motivating factor in entering religious orders became especially salient after the late 1940s when the National Science Foundation initiated a program whereby short study grants were awarded to teachers to continue their educations. Insignificant as it might seem, this decision by NSF had a great influence on the development of religious orders because nuns were included as eligible applicants and many orders encouraged their nuns to apply. Large numbers of them received grants over the next several years, and by the mid 1950s nuns by the thousands attended various Catholic and secular universities during the summer months to obtain advanced degrees. For the first time, nuns left their cloistered environments and associated with students of all sexes and all social class backgrounds and religious persuasions. As these nuns returned to their teaching assignments in the fall, they came back with expanded visions, new ideas, and more professional orientations.

In part, educational opportunities accounted for the large classes that entered religious orders throughout the 1950s and into the early 1960s. It was common during these years for religious orders to have entering groups of sixty to seventy women. Thus, for Catholic girls, nuns provided the role model, and Catholic orders the vehicle, for upward mobility—both out of the working class and away from the restrictions and low status of the traditional wife-mother role.

With the encouragement of Pope Pius XII's mandate to religious superiors in 1950 to educate their nuns on a par with their lay colleagues, entering an order came to virtually guarantee at least a college degree for nuns and often an advanced degree as well. This academic professional preparation meant that nuns were qualified to enter all types of careers that were beginning to open up for women in society.

Nuns as Competent Professional Women

Originally the services provided by nuns were limited to teaching and health care among Catholic immigrants, but by the time of Vatican II the notion of "apostolate" had broadened to include the teaching of secular subjects as well as religion, medical service, social services of all types, and even public service jobs. Commitment within a religious calling was no longer defined in terms of performing a religiously oriented job; any occupation could be "religious" if the person used her profession to better the condition of people.

Regardless of the work a nun chose or was assigned, there has been continuing emphasis within convents that the nun do her job well; that is, she must be as well prepared for her job as possible and view her work as an essential element in her religious commitment. Throughout the centuries, one primary rationale for the celibacy of nuns is that the renunciation of sexual pleasure, emotional commitment to a husband and family, and the time pressures demanded by family life free the nun for total dedication to her work. The corollary of such renunciation was that the nun concentrate upon, and give herself intensely to, her work. The consequence of such commitment has been many highly competent nuns in various professional settings.

At a time when society looked suspiciously at lay women who had careers outside the home, Catholics and non-Catholics alike not only accepted the fact that nuns were career women but came to expect excellent service from them. Catholic schools were valued because of the dedicated and competent nuns who staffed them; Catholic hospitals run by nuns were seen as superior to public or private lay hospitals; social service agencies headed and staffed by nuns were considered some of the best in the country. In many instances nuns paved the way for women into new professional areas. This is the case, for example, with hospital administrators, accrediting boards for various institutions, university professors, scientific researchers, university presidents, and administrators of social work agencies. Today, with affirmative action programs and increasing numbers of women with professional degrees, it is becoming more common to find women in prestigious positions. Long before nondiscriminatory hiring and mandatory quotas, nuns had made their way into these positions. As the Church developed an extensive network of schools, hospitals, orphanages, and other charitable institutions, Catholic nuns administered and ran them. As a result, as Thompson (1986) states, in the nineteenth and early twentieth centuries, nearly the only women who bore responsibility for administering large-scale operations were Catholic nuns. She says they can thus be considered the "first sizeable cohort of female corporate executives."

Nuns as Single Women in Society

One consequence of the recent feminist movement is that single life and childless marriages are becoming more acceptable in American society. Even in the era when single life was generally and strongly frowned upon, people accepted and respected the celibate life of nuns. Not only Catholics, but non-Catholics as well, realized that for some women, at least, it was possible to exist quite happily without an emotional attachment to a man. Thus, when feminists in the late 1960s began to question the "naturalness," desirability, or absolute necessity of permanent relationships with men, society had at least one model of successful single life.

Thus, one point of convergence between nuns and many feminists is the conviction that a woman can live a full and meaningful life without intimate, permanent ties with a male. Over the centuries, nuns have demonstrated that single women can both live fulfilling lives and make valuable contributions to society.

Prior to the popularity of consciousness-raising women's groups in American society, convents were also one of the few places, other than voluntary organizations designed for a specific service in society, where women joined together to support one another. The comraderie and social support that nuns provided one another in their convent lives offered a model for the numerous social support groups that became available to women with the advent of the Women's Movement.

There were, therefore, numerous ways in which Catholic nuns had an impact on the development of feminism in the United States, long before feminism was recognized as a movement ideology. Catholic nuns did not consciously set themselves up as examples of feminism, but the unanticipated consequences of their life-styles articulated with the expressed goals of the Women's Movement.

Early Organizational Confrontations with the Vatican

Shortly after the close of the Second Vatican Council (1965) several religious orders in the United States came into direct conflict with Roman authorities. Although the issues were complex, the basis of the conflict was whether religious orders of women were free to experiment with their structures and life-styles as indicated in the Council's "Decree on the Appropriate Renewal of Religious Life" (as well as the implementation decree issued by Rome in 1966), or whether Roman authorities would place limits on the types of renewal experiments that would be allowed. The original decrees gave religious orders approximately twelve years in which to experiment and present a new constitution to Rome for approval. However, the ink on the decrees was hardly dry before local male Church officials began objecting to specific experiments and demanding that the nuns in their jurisdiction be prohibited from proceeding with self-determined renewal. These officials appealed to Rome for support. The conflict then became polarized between the power of local male authorities and the right of women's religious orders to experiment with renewal programs. The pattern was for Rome to support the clerical structure and order the nuns to submit to their local Church authorities. These orders were then caught in a basic dilemma: if they followed the mandated process of renewal to adapt their structures to their contemporary ministries, they were threatened with the loss of their official canonical status in the Catholic Church. Interestingly, in some cases, the orders were willing to reconstitute themselves as lay organizations rather than submit to local Church officials whom they felt were interfering with their renewal process.

The two most publicized cases of conflict between religious orders and Roman officials occurred with the Glenmary Sisters in Cincinnati and the Immaculate Heart of Mary Sisters in Los Angeles. In September 1965, Cincinnati Archbishop Karl Alter objected to some renewal changes that the Glenmary Sisters were initiating for the purpose of making their ministry among the rural poor in Appalachia more effective. Specifically, the order changed its rules of cloister to allow more contact and interaction with the lay people they were serving. When the archbishop demanded that they return to their convents and was backed by Roman authorities, 50 of the 102 nuns left the order and reconstituted themselves as a lay organization dedicated to Christian service among the Appalachian poor (Weaver, 1986).

While the Glenmary case was the first major departure of American nuns as a protest against objections from a local Church official to their renewal efforts, it was not the most famous and widest publicized case. In 1968 the Immaculate Heart of Mary nuns (IHMs) defied their cardinal by refusing to retract any renewal changes they had initiated in response to Vatican II. The fact that Rome forced them to submit or be ousted from official status as a religious order in the Catholic Church shocked both laity as well as other orders in the Church. Because the IHMs framed their case in feminist terms—that is, their vulnerability to male authorities—it also became a struggle of powerless women against a male-dominated Church hierarchy.

The IHMs, founded in Spain, came to the mission territory of California in 1871 and built schools throughout the area. The nuns rapidly gained a reputation as educated and highly qualified teachers. Professional preparation and certification were values in the order even prior to the Sister Formation Movement and Pope Pius XII's encouragement to educate the sisters. When their local male superior, Cardinal McIntyre, visited the community in 1962 he questioned the community's progressive theological thinking and mandated that they conform to traditional Church teaching or risk their official status in the Church.

During their general chapter meetings in 1967 the IHMs initiated a renewal program in response to Vatican II's mandate that religious orders reevaluate their life-styles and adapt them to modern conditions. The order decided to experiment in five basic areas: greater self-determination in choice of occupation, freedom to substitute contemporary dress for the traditional garb, individual choice in kind, times, and duration of formal prayers, greater representation in the system of government, and significant changes in the socialization of new members.

As a courtesy, Cardinal McIntyre was given a copy of the policy changes. Shortly after receiving them, the cardinal contacted the order and expressed his disapproval. He mandated that the order make substantial changes in them. When the superior general of the order, Mother Mary Humiliata (later known as Sister Anita Caspary) appealed to Rome protesting the interference of the cardinal in their internal affairs, the cardinal toned down his demands somewhat. However, when the order, at a subsequent general chapter, introduced further and more far-reaching policy changes, the cardinal interpreted their actions as a statement of defiance and insisted that if the decrees were not retracted, the nuns must withdraw from the schools in his archdiocese (Ebaugh, 1978).

After the order again appealed to Rome and demonstrated that it was acting within the mandates of the Second Vatican Council for renewal in religious orders, Roman authorities sided, not with the sisters, but with the cardinal and proclaimed that the renewal in the order was causing scandal and had gone too far. Rome ordered the IHMs to comply with the wishes of the cardinal. Rather than submit to a male-dominated authority structure, which the nuns saw as hypocritical, the order split. Fifty nuns opted to comply with Rome, and four hundred left with Sister Anita Caspary to become a new lay group, the Immaculate Heart Community. All four hundred leavers were given dispensations from their vows, and they became the largest group of American nuns to reorganize as a lay community in the Church.

The newly formed community continued the mission and policies that had been established within the IHM order at its renewal chapter. The community, still in existence today, calls itself "a community without walls" and admits married couples, non-Catholics, and divorcees. The community perceives itself as a group of people who share similar values and orientations to life but not similar life-styles or finances (Ebaugh, 1978). Although the new community was initially seen as radical, the astonishing fact is how predictive it was of the direction of changes that would occur within officially recognized religious orders during the succeeding twenty years. It was a case of bad timing because the Church, over the next several decades, became tolerant of many changes that lead to trouble for the IHMs.

Both the Glenmary Sisters and the IHMs clashed with male authorities who objected to nuns governing their own lives, even though the male-dominated Council had, in principle, not only condoned but also encouraged nuns to reevaluate their organizational structures and experiment with renewed structures that would make religious orders more relevant in the mid twentieth century. The IHMs, in particular, framed the conflict they experienced in feminist terms; in the prologue to their renewal constitution, they stated:

> Women around the world, young and old, are playing decisive roles in public life, changing their world, developing new life styles. What is significant about this new power for women is not that it will always be for the good, nor that it will always edify, but that there can be no reversing of it now. Women who want to serve and who are capable of service have already given evidence that they can no longer uncritically accept the judgment of others as to where and how that service ought to be extended. American religious women want to be in the mainstream of this new, potentially fruitful, and inevitable bid for self-determination by women. (Decree of the Ninth General Chapter of the Sisters of the Immaculate Heart of Mary)

The response of American nuns in support of the Glenmary Sisters, as well as IHMs, was as surprising as the bold actions of the orders themselves in standing up to Roman authorities. Not only did both orders receive hundreds of supportive letters from nuns around the country, but Catholic newspapers such as the *National Catholic Reporter* printed letters and editorials from nuns in support of the firm stance of the orders against the male Church hierarchy.

In supporting the position of the Glenmary Sisters and the IHMs, American nuns were sending a message to Rome that the days of blind submission to male authority were over and that religious orders were taking seriously the challenge of Vatican II for the self-renewal of religious orders. Given the traditional submissiveness of nuns in the Catholic Church, it is possible that the Council "fathers" did not anticipate the creativity, readiness, and strength of Catholic nuns, especially in the United States, to effect the kinds of renewal that occurred. American nuns were clearly ready for greater colleagiality and recognition in the Church. The challenge of the Council simply opened the floodgates and provided legitimation for the self-determination that became a hallmark of the renewal process in American orders.

The Outspoken Feminism of Nuns Today

Unlike the unwitting feminism of traditional nuns and the isolated cases of organizational confrontation between some religious orders and Rome, today's nuns are outspokenly feminist, in their language, their mission statements and goals, the causes that are important to them, the types of jobs they are seeking, and the value they place upon their collective power as women in the Church. In this section I discuss the contemporary feminism of American nuns in four areas: withdrawal from parish work, involvement in social justice issues affecting women, articulating women's issues in mission statements, and grappling with the current conservative reactions of Roman authorities to renewal in American orders.

The Dual Labor Market in Catholic Parishes

During the 1970s many Catholic nuns left parochial school teaching and took up all types of jobs in the parish structure. Parish ministry became a highly sought after occupation and was seen as central to shaping the post-council renewal that was beginning to take place within parishes throughout the Church. Between 1968 and 1982 the percentage of American nuns employed in pastoral ministry and in parish religious education more than doubled (Neal, 1984). At the same time, there was a significant decline in ownership by religious orders of the places where nuns worked (Neal, 1984).

The shift from parochial school settings where nuns both administered and staffed the schools, as well as from congregationally owned institutions, into parish ministry involved unanticipated frustrations for nuns owing to the dual labor market that existed in Catholic parishes. According to dual labor market theory (LaMagdeleine, 1986; Ritzer and Walczak, 1986; Salaman, 1981), occupational structures are composed of primary and secondary sectors. In the higher-status primary labor market, employment is stable and rewarding, provides opportunities for career advancement, and offers appropriate salaries. Workers in the secondary sector, by contrast, are poorly paid, have virtually no chance for career advancement, and have little authority and few opportunities to move into the primary sector. LaMagdeleine (1986) as well as Wittberg (1989) use dual market theory to differentiate male and female roles within parish structures, describing priestly male roles within parish structures as primary sector roles and subordinate female roles as part of the secondary sector.

As Heslin (1983), Joseph et al. (1980), and Wittberg (1989) demonstrate in their studies of new ministries for nuns, the stress of working in a male-dominated, hierarchical church structure is a source of great job dissatisfaction for nuns in parish settings. The lack of power and upward mobility in parish and diocesan staff positions form the source of this dissatisfaction.

While nuns are frequently more qualified than male clergy in some parish ministries, such as theological education and counseling positions, and despite the professional competence with which they usually perform their jobs, because of their ascribed status as women, they are blocked from upward mobility into positions such as pastor or priest. Wallace's (1992) data on female pastoral administrators show clearly that blocked mobility is the major source of job dissatisfaction for this group. She describes female pastoral administrators who expressed great frustration at being allowed to prepare converts for baptism, new communicants to receive communion in the Church, laity to participate in liturgical worship, and engaged couples for the sacrament of marriage, and yet they are forbidden by Church law to follow through in terms of performing the liturgical ritual associated with these events. Even in those cases where women are allowed to be pastors of parishes because of the dearth of male clergy (Wallace, 1992), there are stringent limits within which female pastors must operate; namely, they cannot perform the rituals associated with membership in that exclusive club of male priests within the Catholic Church.

In addition to being excluded from the priestly functions of liturgical rituals, the phenomenon of female administrators in charge of parishes is still very rare in the American Church and has occurred only recently with the drastic decline in male clergy (Schoenherr and Sorensen, 1982). The more common case is for female pastoral workers to have male priest administrators as bosses. In Wittberg's (1989) study, nuns working in parishes under clergy supervision felt more job dissatisfaction because of blocked mobility and powerlessness than nuns working in institutions owned and/or operated by their orders.

As more and more nuns experienced low status and relative powerlessness in their parish ministries, they began to define their dissatisfaction in feminist terms; that is, they realized that blocked mobility and subordinate positions were owing to their status as women in the Church. Simultaneously, they began to identify not just as nuns in the Church with problems unique to vowed religious women, but with all Catholic women who are structurally limited in terms of mobility. In the past ten years, nuns have become some of the most vocal feminists heard in the Church, speaking out not just for greater freedom for nuns but for all women. When Theresa Kane, president of the Leadership Conference of Women Religious, greeted the pope in Washington in the late 1970s she urged him "to be mindful of the intense suffering and pain that is part of the life of many women" and encouraged him to hear the call of women to be included in all ministries of the Church (Carpenter, 1980). In doing this, she was representing the feminist voice of Catholic women. The lack of response by the pope, as well as the intense criticism of her action by the official Church hierarchy (Weaver, 1986), became symbolic for the Catholic feminist movement of the subordination and submissiveness expected of women by the Church.

While many nuns, during the decade of the 1970s, flocked into parish ministry, during the 1980s they began to withdraw from this work, disillusioned by the powerlessness, subjugation, and frustration of dealing with male cleric superiors. Several studies (Joseph et al., 1980; Fox, 1986; Wittberg, 1989) have found that ambiguity of function, overlapping roles, and lack of clarity in job titles are prime reasons for dissatisfaction and quitting. As Wittberg (1989) points out, failing to define roles or areas of responsibility can be used by pastors as a means of preventing the establishment of separate bases of power among those who work for them. The facts that those in authority are inevitably male pastors and those without power and frustrated by the system are women define the situation as discriminatory; the issue is thus a feminist one.

The Social Activism of American Nuns

Beginning with the Civil Rights Movement in the 1960s, American nuns were involved in almost every subsequent social movement in the United States. Against the wishes of many conservative bishops, hundreds of nuns took part in the civil rights marches and sit-ins in Alabama and Mississippi. In the course of these radicalizing activities, many nuns in this country became aware of institutional discrimination and the need to build social structures that assure equality.

When the Mexican American immigrant grape pickers, led by Cesar Chavez, demonstrated for higher wages and better working conditions throughout California and the Southwest and called for a grape boycott, Catholic nuns were leaders in the movement. Convents throughout the country, as well as school and hospital cafeterias staffed by nuns, stopped serving grapes and grape products.

Several controversial figures who have been arrested in connection with the Sanctuary Movement to provide assistance to illegal immigrants into this country from Latin and Central America are current and former Catholic nuns. In fact, throughout religious orders today, including the Sisters of Service, a major policy issue involves the decision whether to open local convents, as well as motherhouses, as places of sanctuary. The provision of such shelter is still illegal, even though several cases are being appealed within the judicial system. For religious orders that decide to proceed with providing sanctuary, it is one of the first times in which they are taking a policy stand in direct defiance of civil law.

Nuns were also very active in the peace movement that protested the war in Vietnam. National television showed nuns among the peace demonstrators on campuses across the country and in marches down Pennsylvania Avenue. The peace movement caught the attention of both older, more traditionally garbed nuns as well as younger nuns dressed in modified habits.

There were few, if any, official objections from Church authorities regarding the involvement of nuns in social justice issues during the 1960s and 1970s, but the decade of the 1980s was very different for activist nuns as well as their religious orders. During the 1980s a number of individual nuns, as well as religious orders, were censored by Rome for radical social activities. Weaver (1986) explains the change in the Vatican's reactions in terms of the types of issues that nuns were protesting. In the past ten years these issues revolved around structural change rather than the rights of individuals and, as Weaver argues, "the closer a group gets to issues of structural change, externally, through social justice work and political involvement, or, internally, by way of challenging institutional structures, the more dangerous they appear to authorities and the more they draw Vatican opprobrium."

Many nuns who have been censored by Rome in the past few years are members of the Sisters of Mercy of the Union (RSMs). Sister Theresa Kane, who challenged the pope on the issue of women's ordination during his visit to the United States, was a member of that order. Agnes Mary Mansour was given the ultimatum by the pope to resign from her post as director of social services for the state of Michigan or to leave the religious order in which she had been a nun for thirty years because her agency provided abortions for women who wanted them. Arlene Violet, Republican nominee for attorney general of Rhode Island, was forbidden from running for public office as a nun. She took a "temporary leave" from her order while she pursued the race. Elizabeth Morancy, a three-term Democratic member of the Rhode Island House of Representatives, wanted to remain in her order while serving in political office; however, because of opposition from Church authorities, she asked to be dispensed from her vows in order to stay in politics (Weaver, 1986).

These various cases, all occurring within the same order, have highlighted the conflict between the order and Vatican officials because the order has tended to support the individuals involved. However, Rome has put great pressure upon the order to discipline its members and assure that they comply with the ultimatums of the Vatican. With the exception of Theresa Kane, rather than cause further trouble for the order, the individuals involved have left the order.

Weaver (1986) suggests that perhaps Rome singled out this particular order for harassment and ultimatums to show other American orders what can happen if they challenge religious authority. Many nuns, typified by the nuns in this particular order, are committed to both social justice and structural change. However, in confronting the traditional Church, embodied in the reactionary and conservative reaction of the Vatican in these recent cases, they are challenging the world's oldest and most entrenched living bureaucracy.

Feminist Commitments in Contemporary
Mission Statements

Many of the new constitutions currently being submitted to Rome by religious orders of women in this country explicitly state a commitment to feminist issues. The Sisters of Service order, for instance, states in its mission statement that it is committed to "standing with the materially poor and the powerless by . . . furthering the transformation of oppressive systems by promoting the human liberation from ignorance, racism, sexism, and economic deprivation" and "expanding participation of all people, especially girls and women, in ecclesial and civic life" (Acts of Chapter, 1987).

In her analysis of the new constitutions that more than five hundred religious orders of women are in process of submitting to Rome for approval, Neal (1990) notes that a theme running through all their goal statements is the eradication of all social oppression, including sexist structures that prohibit women from full participation in their societies. Neal says that the primary focus of ministry in these various documents is "the elimination of the causal factors of poverty and of related injustices." Throughout the constitutions, religious orders express the elimination of sexual injustices, along with social class and racial discrimination, as primary goals of the religious order in the contemporary world.

The Value of Canonical Status in the Church

The final issue that many contemporary religious orders are being challenged to face is that of maintaining official status within the conservative, male-dominated Church. To maintain official status as an approved religious order, each order must submit a revised constitution to the Congregation for Religious Institutes of Consecrated Life (CICL), an administrative department of the Vatican that oversees religious orders to assure their harmony with Church life. Recently, a number of orders have had their revised constitutions returned with a "revise and resubmit" notice. In other words, the committee objected to portions of the document and refused to approve it without changes. Some of these suggestions have run counter to decisions made by the duly elected representatives of the order. This can be a serious problem if the suggested changes contradict the structures the nuns see as necessary for carrying out their mission.

The fact that the Vatican committee consists of male clergy, most of them non-Americans, further ignites the ire of American nuns who feel that their unique cultural experience is foreign to the committee. Also, the fact that male clerics have the authority to make decisions regarding the commitments and life-style of religious women is a sore issue for the more radical feminists in these orders.

Although some members in religious orders favor renouncing official status as a recognized religious order in the Church and becoming a lay institute over which Rome has less control, others continue to value their status as vowed nuns in the Church and feel that institutional affiliation with the official Church is important to their ministry. The pattern has been for orders to acquiesce to Rome by making their formal statements so general that they do not threaten the conservative, European male hierarchy and then to proceed to interpret the statements to encompass the types of works and life-styles appropriate for modern American women.

In conclusion, nuns in the United States have been central figures in the feminist movement. In pre–Vatican II days, this influence was primarily unwitting: Catholic nuns represented the only role alternative for immigrant, working-class girls who were otherwise expected to be dutiful wives and mothers. Entering a convent was not only acceptable in these Catholic immigrant communities, but it gave status to families whom God chose to produce offspring for special service in the Church. Entering a convent was a viable avenue for upward social mobility because nuns were educated, professional women in a society in which few women had such opportunities.

Religious orders became more democratic, open institutions after the Council, and nuns became more vocal in the Church; their feminism, therefore, became more overt. As both orders and individuals within these orders, nuns began to challenge their submissive status as well as a structure that operated to oppress women. The fact that most revised constitutions submitted to Rome for approval explicitly articulate the elimination of sexual oppression as a goal indicates the consciousness raising that has occurred within religious orders. What happens next to the feminism of American nuns depends on Rome's response to these constitutions and the religious orders' response to opposition.

CHAPTER 10

Membership Morale

The literature on declining organizations predicts that membership morale tends to sag and high turnover results as people realize that the organization is in trouble (Behn, 1978; Levine, 1979; Whetten, 1980a). Members tend to become preoccupied with how change will affect them and eagerly seek out information that relates to the current state of the organization. Information seeking becomes a top priority with members while the administration, simultaneously, tends to withhold information from members as long as possible in order to avoid panic, stress, and loss of commitment (Greenhalgh, 1978, 1983).

The above reactions to decline, well documented in the organizational literature, do not characterize the response of members in the Sisters of Service. Although the membership is well aware of the signs of decline and talk of being part of a dying organization is commonplace, morale remains quite high, despite daily reminders of few new recruits, rising median age, and the group's financial woes.

Acceptance of Organizational Decline

Perhaps one reason for the upbeat spirit in the order, under conditions that could easily lead to demoralization, is the bold decision of the administration in the spring of 1990 to make organizational decline a public issue rather than shielding members from information. The order had a ten- to fifteen-year history of openness with members in regard to membership statistics and finances, but the legal issue that was raised in the fall of 1989 of reincorporation as a memberless corporation pinpointed the issue of the order's future. Although the administration, acting upon advice from its attorney to reduce the legal liabilities of the corporation, raised the issue to the membership, it anticipated neither the strength nor the nature of the discussion that ensued. The necessity of specifying what would happen to the assets of the order in the event it ceased to exist caused members to ask whether the administration was anticipating its eventual end. When the administration realized the concern of members, it decided to confront the issue forthrightly and challenge members to face the possibility of demise in the light of virtually no new recruits, the relatively high number of defections over the past two decades, the alarmingly high median age of members, and the financial difficulties of an aging membership.

In the numerous group discussions that took place regarding organizational decline, members of the order began to articulate and share their assessments and feelings regarding decline. Some members expressed fear of the future and disappointment with the course of events in the order, but with the help of several articles that placed decline in a positive light, most members began to articulate an acceptance of the situation and express a positive stance in terms of what it could mean for the order.

By the time I interviewed members the summer following the spring discussions, the morale in the order was quite positive. The most common response to the interview question regarding feelings about the future of the order is exemplified in the following quote from a nun in her early fifties: "People don't live forever and neither do organizations. There was a time when we were needed in the Church, but perhaps that is not the case any more. Perhaps other types of groups will take over those needs. Our job is to die gracefully and not hold on to something that is no longer needed."

Several other members expressed the challenge for the order to accept its death and for members to concentrate on having meaningful lives while the order lasts. "It is not important for the congregation to last, but what is important is what and who we are now." Living a full and meaningful life as individuals and presenting a positive image of the order is a major goal for many members such as this forty-eight-year-old sister: "We may be dying, but we'll go out in glory, enjoying our lives the best we can. If we die as a group, it's O.K. It means our charism is no longer needed in the Church through this particular lifestyle."

A commonly heard expression in the order is one the members picked up from an article they shared in group discussions. As one member paraphrased it, "We had a definite place in the traditional Church and served her well. Things have changed, and the Church needs other kinds of groups now, including more associations for laity who are becoming leaders in the Church. I say, let's go out gracefully and the last one turn out the lights."

One article used in discussions within the order was written by Patricia Wittberg (1988); she compares the recent decline in religious orders with the accelerating rate of decline among organizations of all types in our modern world. She argues that organizational decline is part of the evolutionary process within organizations and that it does not necessarily indicate failure of the organization but simply the fact that it has outlived or perhaps even accomplished its purpose. She further suggests that perhaps religious orders can be models of "redemptive letting go" of institutional forms that are outdated and must be abandoned for new forms to arise.

In the order's discussion groups the Wittberg article was perhaps the most influential source for posing organizational decline in a positive light. The article provided ways for members to both justify the decline process to outsiders and define and cope with the process in their own lives. The fact that the entire membership read and discussed the article provided an acceptable group framework for articulating and responding to the decline and demise that members were witnessing.

The Process of Decline

Despite the fact that most members came to accept the inevitability of organizational decline, the process of living in a dying organization is still painful. As one member said, "A dying institution is not depressing, but the process of dying is depressing." Other members expressed the process as "scary" because of the many unknowns that must be faced as membership declines.

For the older members, the pain is experienced mainly in terms of seeing something to which they have dedicated their lives as no longer viable. In fact, while many older nuns admit that things have to change in the order, they hold onto the hope that a new form of religious life will emerge within the old structures. For this group, the associate program holds much hope because of the large numbers of people who are joining the order as associates. Among these older members, there is much talk of the continuance of the order's charism through the associate program.

For those members in their fifties and sixties the issue of organizational survival seems less important than ways to maximize their service here and now in the Church, as well as maintaining feelings of bondedness with the group. There is little concern or fear of the future, even though this group faces retirement within the next quarter-century. They are convinced that the order has enough capital resources in land and buildings to have the means to take care of them in retirement. There is a tremendous sense of identification with the order in this group, even though many of them are very independent in terms of their careers and involvements. This cohort experienced socialization at a time when the order was a total institution, separated from society and focused upon forging a group identity among its members. The result of the traditional socialization practices is evident in the intense identification this cohort has with both the order as a whole and fellow members in like age cohorts.

Among this age group there are feelings of nostalgia and loss of a life-style that has been meaningful to them. As one nun put it, "I don't worry about the financial future as much as I feel a real deep sadness that all the people that are important to me that are older than me will be dead and there will be nobody behind me not just to take care of me but to carry on something to which I have given my life. It's like not having children to pass things on to, nobody to inherit what is important to me in my lifetime."

Those members under fifty, referred to as the "young sisters," are most unsure of the future and who are "drawing lines in the sand" in terms of the conditions under which they will stay with the order. Although many of them are convinced that the order will not survive their lifetimes, they are not ready to leave because they value the fact that they are with a group of women who have similar goals and purposes in life. For this reason, they are comfortable in the order. Yet, as one young nun said, "I feel foolish, in some ways, sticking with a dying group. I wonder if I'm just hanging on to things too long. But there is a richness of spirit here that means something to me, and I am not ready to give it up."

At the same time, many of the younger members fear that others in their cohort may leave, which would radically affect the nature of communal living for them. For many in this age group, there is less identification with the order as a whole than with members in their general age cohort. Community, for them, is experienced in terms of friendship and solidarity with other younger members so that the departure of significant others would affect their sense of communal belonging.

The younger nuns also feel the responsibility placed upon them to support a growing proportion of elderly members. As one person in her twenties put it, "In the congregation, each one of us needs to care for many old people, not just one parent, and the sense of responsibility sometimes is too much." There is also some resentment among the younger members that the bulk of administrative time and attention is spent on retirement issues, especially financial concerns regarding the care of the large elderly membership. The young members feel that more attention and resources are being spent on the retired than on those who are supporting them.

Despite the fears and feelings of loss that members experience as they face the decline of the order, the overall spirit of acceptance, optimism, peace, and satisfaction with the renewal that has taken place in the order is evident among members of all ages. Even though members are aware of the serious organizational problems, they are happy with the greater freedom and independence allowed them in their own careers and lives.

Feminist Response to the Male-Dominated Church

Increasingly, over the past several decades, the Sisters of Service have become more and more vocal as feminists within the Catholic Church. This trend has been evident in the recent general assemblies in the order. More and more nuns are complaining about the blocked opportunity structures for women in the Church, in terms of both liturgical involvement and positions of authority. The earlier enthusiasm associated with expanding job opportunities within parishes has given way to disillusionment as nuns involved in these jobs realize that they must report to male administrators and that they themselves are prohibited from ever moving into these positions. In addition, regardless of the theological training they receive, nuns realize that they are not allowed to say Mass and officiate at their public rituals. During the assemblies, nuns prepare and deliver the scriptural readings, constitute the choir and musical presentations, lead religious processions, and even deliver the sermon. However, when it comes to the "holiest" and most central part of the Mass, namely, the communion service, they must step aside and allow a male priest to officiate. Usually, he is the only male present at the ceremony and joins the group only temporarily for the celebration of Mass. He is an "outsider" in that he has not been part of the community gathering or rituals of solidarity that precede and follow the Mass. During the past several general assemblies, more and more nuns have commented upon and condemned the gender inequities made apparent in this regulation.

Many nuns in the order are also involved in various women's groups throughout the Church, groups that are raising consciousness of the gender stratification in the Church and beginning to organize in protest. Some nuns take a reformist posture and argue that the best way to change the structure is from within, but others question whether professing vows in such an institution is condoning a discriminatory institution. Recently, a member of the order left for the explicit reason that she felt she could not be part of an institution that discriminated against women. Interestingly, the reaction of most people in the order was deep respect and admiration for her action.

The fact that the order openly discussed and struggled with the dilemma that would arise if Rome refused to approve its new constitutions is an indication that the issue of compliance with a male-dominated authority structure is important for the order. There was conflict over how far the order should be willing to compromise in the event of a refusal from Rome. The fact that the constitutions were approved dissipated the issue for the time being.

The increasing activism in the order in regard to feminist issues is strongly supported by most people in the order. Almost all those members that I interviewed were proud that the order was becoming more cognizant of and supportive of women's issues.

Given the fact that the Sisters of Service, like all female religious orders, operates within a male-dominated Church causes mixed reactions in some members regarding the future of religious orders. As one nun put it, "Maybe religious orders of women are no longer a good thing in the Church because we dedicate our lives to a Church that treats us like second-class citizens. Until we have all the rights of men in the Church, why should we publicly represent a Church that discriminates against women?" In a subtle way, the demise of religious orders is a consequence of the gender stratification system in the Church. At least some nuns in the order feel that religious orders are no longer viable in a Church that will not grant equal power and recognition to women. They feel that serious conflict with Church authorities is inevitable as long as women religious insist on organizational autonomy and Rome refuses to grant equal rights to women.

Rejection of What It Might Take to Survive Organizationally

Beginning with Kanter's elaboration of commitment mechanisms in intentional communities (Kanter, 1972), there has been a growing sociological literature specifying the conditions under which intentional groups are most likely to survive (Kanter, 1972; Zablocki, 1980; Wittberg, 1991). Major predictors of survival include boundary maintenance, uniformity of life-style, common beliefs and rituals, sacrifice, and mortification. I briefly discuss each mechanism and show how post–Vatican II orders have deliberately renounced each of them in their renewal process.

To survive, intentional communities must differentiate clearly between insiders and outsiders and must establish structures to assure that insiders associate with each other and use each other as a reference group. When boundaries become fluid, both physically and socially, it is difficult to reinforce group identity and norms.

Uniformity of life-style, including dress, daily schedule, material possessions, and common rules and regulations, deemphasizes individual needs and differences and accentuates the identity of belonging to the group. Likewise, sharing common beliefs and rituals creates a sense of group identity and reinforces a sense of group history.

Through the process of mortification a person "dies" to his or her individual self in order to be reborn to a new identity, one shared with members of the group. In addition to socialization and initiation rituals that symbolize this death and rebirth, most successful intentional groups require mortification rituals of confession, self-criticism, and the asking of forgiveness by the group.

Finally, successful communities require great acts of sacrifice by members, including celibacy, renunciation of family, property, and monetary gifts, abstention from bodily pleasures such as alcohol and drugs, and the discipline of early rising, hard work, and material disadvantages. Such sacrifices enhance commitment by convincing both the individual and the others that the costs are worth the rewards of being a member. As a result, rewards of group membership are accentuated in order to justify the sacrifices required for membership. Sacrifice reinforces a sense that membership is highly valued.

It is noteworthy that all the above mechanisms of commitment characterized pre–Vatican II religious orders and were integral parts of what made them total institutions. The renewal of Vatican II, however, defined these disciplinary and isolating structures as outdated in the twentieth century and offensive to modern recruits. In an effort to make religious life more appealing to young women and to make it more relevant in the modern world, these outdated structures with their emphasis upon renunciation and deindividuation were rejected in favor of more democratic, open, individually oriented structures. The paradox, however, is that the modernization in religious orders after the Council was accompanied by high rates of membership defection and decreased entrance rates of new recruits. Rather than having the effect of making religious life more appealing to modern women, at least in the United States, the renewal lead to decreased numbers of religious women.

Based on what we know about commitment in intentional communities, one way to maximize organizational survival would be for religious orders to return to a more autocratic, uniform, discipline-oriented system where individuality is subjugated to group norms. There are two problems with this solution. First, once people experience more freedom, it is very difficult to take it from them without protest and revolution. Doubtless, if such a move were attempted in the Sisters of Service, many nuns would leave the order. The Sisters of Service follow a pattern that Wittberg (1988) observes in many orders today: that orders have chosen the prospect of decline and extinction rather than risk a return to what they see as psychologically destructive group survival mechanisms of the past.

Second, given the new theology of Vatican II, it is unlikely that religious orders would value the return to traditional structures to assure survival. Basically, commitment to the spirit and renewal introduced by the Council is more important to most nuns than survival of their particular order. In the process of renewal religious women became more committed to the renewed Church and the spirit of Vatican II than to any particular institution in that Church.

Repeatedly, in my interviews with Sisters of Service, I heard nuns say that they wanted to see the charism of their order continued in some form, but not necessarily as it has been institutionalized in the present order. As members face the fact that the order probably will not survive, they are shifting their commitment from the order as it now exists to assuring that the spirit and mission will survive in other forms, especially among the people who have been served by the order for many years.

CHAPTER 11

A Process Model
of the Demise
# of Convents

Three major themes have provided the framework for this book: (1) a description of how the decline process in religious orders does not follow the patterns predicted in the organizational decline literature; (2) the contention that certain exogenous factors set in motion the renewal process in religious orders and influenced the ideological and structural changes that were initiated, changes that eventually lead to their demise; and (3) the fact that religious orders were confronted with a series of organizational dilemmas for which there were no viable solutions. The data that I have presented to document the decline of religious orders, as well as my argument that demise is virtually inevitable, have been interpreted in terms of these three major themes. In this final chapter I summarize the basic arguments, relate the themes to one another, and describe the basic dilemma that I contend will eventuate in the demise of the institution in this country.

Organizational Decline: Religious Orders as a Deviant Case

During the past fifteen years there has been a growing literature on organizational decline. On the basis of numerous studies of declining organizations, it is possible to make certain predictions regarding the decline process. These predictions include centralization of authority, the internal reallocation of resources, fear of risk taking, intraorganizational turf battles, environmental manipulation, and the loss of morale on the part of members in the organization.

In terms of the case study described in this book, these predictions have not materialized, at least not to the extent described in the organizational decline literature. I briefly describe the discrepancies in terms of the case study and posit an explanation for why the case study order deviates from the normal patterns of decline.

Routinely, administrators in declining organizations tend to tighten the reigns of authority to avoid the alienation and defections that frequently result when members fear organizational problems. Rather than inform members of problems and involve them in the struggle to survive, administrators tend to make the tough decisions themselves and inform members after the fact. During the past several decades, however, religious orders have opted for a different course, with authority becoming increasingly more democratic and communication channels more open than in the traditional, stable system.

Likewise, rather than reallocating resources from external concerns to internal affairs in order to address issues of decline, the Sisters of Service intensified the resources they committed to external works. This was especially the case in terms of subsidizing members who wanted to be employed in poverty settings where they received low pay and few benefits. In fact, in the past ten years the order has made a commitment to "stand with the materially poor" and to serve them regardless of adequate remuneration.

Related to their commitment to serve the poor, as well as greater autonomy in occupational choice, the order has not only allowed but also encouraged extensive occupational diversity. As a result, the order substantially lost control over members in terms of job assignments, uniformity of living situations, and individual finances. The order opted for greater individualism rather than an authoritarian system, even though the risks of defection and decreased commitment to the group are greater in a more open system.

In addition, motivated by issues of social justice, the order began to take public stands on issues related to the poor, civil rights, migrant workers, environmental issues, and women's rights. In taking these stances, the order risked criticism from both the conservative Church hierarchy as well as more conservative members within the Church body.

Turf battles in the order have focused not so much on the allocation of organizational resources as on conflicts between those members favoring change and modernization and the more conservative members resistant to renewal. Although these turf battles have subsided, they are not over; in fact, they continue to arise around various sensitive issues.

Religious orders have lost their unique niche in the Catholic Church, with the decline of parochial schools and the increased role of the laity in the Church, but they have not made a serious attempt to redefine a niche for themselves. As a result, they are experiencing organizational anomie in terms of articulating a corporate mission. Given their occupational diversity and their commitment to individualism in terms of occupations, living situations, and involvement in social activities, it is virtually impossible to define goals except in broad, general terms. Members are unwilling to give up their autonomy and diversity in favor of uniformity.

Unlike the loss of membership morale that usually accompanies decline within organizations, members in the case study order have, on the whole, not become demoralized or cynical. Rather, they are happy with the types of changes that the organization has made and stand firm in their desire that renewal and change continue. In fact, most members are satisfied and content both in their jobs and with the directions of change. Even the realization of decline and the threat of extinction have not demoralized them or caused those who remain to make active plans to leave the organization.

A major reason that members in the order are not demoralized is that they realize the changes made within the order were necessary as a response to the renewal mandated by the Council. Prior to Vatican II, even though every Catholic was supposed to be an example of Christian witness, this role was assigned in a unique way to men and women within religious orders in the Church. Vatican II made it clear that nuns were not clerics in the Church but part of the laity and that every baptized lay person has the mission to spread the kingdom of God on earth. Nuns were dethroned, in a sense, and redefined as laity. The changes instituted within religious orders followed from this redefinition. The cloister and strict boundary maintenance gave way to more open structures that not only permitted association with the laity but also actively encouraged it.

The purpose of religious orders shifted from specific types of service in the Church to that of living the Christian life as fully as possible, a purpose shared with laity in the Church. The fact that nuns take the vows of poverty, chastity, and obedience makes their Christian living assume a unique form; however, the vows are not seen as a higher form of Christianity, they simply offer a different expression than married life.

As the goals of religious orders have become more and more amorphous and less differentiated from Catholicism in general, religious orders have lost their unique status in the Church. Rather than resent the loss of status, nuns, on the whole, have been supportive of the renewal initiated by Vatican II and active at the forefront of supporting and instituting the changes created by the Council. As a result, the survival of their particular order, or religious orders in general, became less important to American nuns than commitment to the course of renewal in the Church.

In summary, even though religious orders are definitely in decline, it is obvious that they are not responding to organizational decline in the same way that characterizes other types of organizations that have been studied. Why are they different? The major reason lies in the type of organization they are: namely, a normative, value-driven institution committed to promulgating a specific approach to life. The primary focus of religious orders, in both the past and present, is to witness to a Christian way of life.

The studies of organizational decline have focused primarily upon profit-making organizations (see Cameron et al., 1988, and Staw et al., 1981, for a summary of these studies), public bureaucracies (see Wynne, 1983; Hirschhorn, 1983), school systems (Cameron and Ulrich, 1986; Freeman and Hannan, 1975), and occupational associations (Akers and Campbell, 1970). The predictions regarding organizational decline have been based on these types of organizations. In addition, the work of Kanter (1972) on successful communes has shed additional light on factors that differentiate successful from unsuccessful communes. There has been little empirical research regarding decline in normative organizations (Etzioni, 1961), namely, organizations that rely on normative power for control and that elicit commitment from members to the goals of the organization. In addition to religious groups, normative organizations include patriotic societies, civil rights organizations, human aid societies, support groups whose purpose is to provide comraderie and a sense of solidarity for the members, and various voluntary organizations. I propose that the theory of organizational decline used to analyze the specific decline in religious orders of women in this book is applicable to other types of normative organizations. At the end of this chapter I suggest ways in which the theory is generalizable to other organizations.

A Process Model of Change in Religious Orders

During the past thirty years a number of factors, external to the orders themselves, came together in time and space and lead to specific structural changes within religious orders of women in the United States. These structural changes, in turn, interacted in such a way as to make the demise of the institution virtually inevitable. Although some external factors were present in earlier historical eras, never before had the exact confluence of factors been present. There have been cycles of change within religious orders in previous centuries, but the unique congruence of factors at this particular period of history makes survival of the institution unlikely.

In this section I summarize the process of change that has occurred within religious orders during the past three decades in terms of (1) the exogenous factors that came together historically, beginning in the 1960s, (2) the structural changes that occurred within religious orders in response to these factors, and (3) how these structural changes have lead to the demise of the institution. Figure 11.1 depicts graphically the processual theory upon which my argument rests.

The six exogenous factors that occurred together in the United States during the 1960s were: Vatican II, expanding opportunities for women, declining birth rates, the feminist movement, increased credentialism by professional associations, and changes in both governmental programs and the insurance industry. Of these factors, the two that had greatest impact upon religious orders of women were Vatican II and expanding opportunities for women, especially in terms of careers.

Vatican II

One major theme of the Second Vatican Council was the introduction of colleagiality and subsidiarity into the authority structure of the Church. Colleagiality was interpreted as greater participation by both

FIGURE 11.1
Process Model for the Demise of Religious Orders in the United States

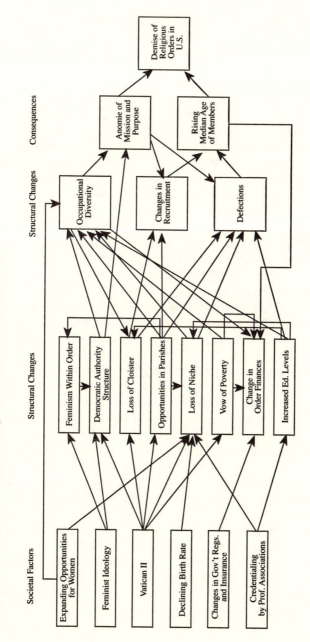

clergy and laity in the governance of the Church. The traditional hierarchical system gave way to greater democracy on all levels of Church governance. The handmaiden concept, subsidiarity, meant that decisions should be made at the level at which they are implemented.

The new approach to authority, mandated by the Council, had two major effects within religious orders. First, the hierarchical, autocratic system of authority that was exercised in religious orders for centuries gave way to a more democratic authority structure in which members participated in the governance of their own lives. Second, in accordance with the mandate of the Council, every member was involved in the process of renewal that took place in religious orders in the decade following the Council. In the course of the renewal process, nuns learned to take responsibility for both their own lives and the order in which they were members.

In addition to changes in the authority structure, the Council also insisted that religious orders adapt their structures to the modern world. As religious orders went about the task of self-evaluation, it became obvious that the traditional cloister was no longer relevant to their mission of witnessing among the laity in the Church. In addition, the Council had defined nuns as laity. To take their place among other laity in the Church and to be witnesses of Christian living among the laity, religious orders saw the necessity of eradicating those barriers of cloister that separated them from others in the Church. Religious orders also hoped to attract more recruits by "humanizing" religious life and discontinuing those practices that had no direct bearing upon witnessing to Christ's kingdom on earth. As a result, the cloister was eradicated, and more open and fluid boundaries between religious convents and the outside world were established.

Along with the introduction of greater democracy into Church government, the Council also raised the status and role of laity in the Church by defining the Church as "the People of God." The laity was encouraged to participate in the life of the Church at all levels. Commissions, councils, and jobs were developed, both at the diocesan and parish levels, to involve the laity in the work of the Church. Education programs were established to teach the "new theology" of post–Vatican II, as well as to train lay people to participate in the activities of the parish. Parish ministry was no longer defined as a role for male clergy. Because nuns were well educated and had training as teachers, they became a major pool for recruiting parish workers. No longer were nuns involved solely in parochial schools; many nuns became involved both in adult education in the parishes as well as the religious education of the increasing numbers of Catholic children who attended public schools.

Pope John XXIII's call for renewal and adaptation of the Church to the modern world challenged the ghetto mentality that characterized the mid-twentieth-century Catholic Church in both Europe and the United States. Prior to the Council, all Catholic parents were expected to make every effort to send their children to Catholic parochial schools rather than subject them to the dangers of secular education. The Council's ameliorative attitude toward the secular world, coupled with more vibrant religious education programs in the parishes, made it more acceptable to send Catholic children to public schools. In addition, the cost of parochial schools became prohibitive for many Catholic parents as well as the parishes that supported them.

As Catholic schools declined, religious orders lost their unique niche in the Church. For at least one hundred years in this country, parochial schools were able to survive because of the relatively cheap labor provided by Catholic nuns. Shortly after the Council, there were more lay teachers in parochial schools than nun-teachers. The unique mission of educating Catholic youth was no longer the primary purpose for religious orders.

Finally, Vatican II redefined the vow of poverty for religious women by its insistence that the Church and its representatives stand with the materially poor in society. No longer was communal sharing sufficient as an expression of poverty. Nuns, as well as the Church as an institution, were called both to see the value of living poorly as Christ lived and to work to better social conditions for the disadvantaged in the world.

Vatican II, therefore, had far-reaching consequences for religious orders. Authority structures became more democratic. The cloister gave way to open boundaries between insiders and outsiders. Job opportunities for nuns opened up within Catholic parishes. The expansion of parish jobs for nuns, coupled with the eradication of the ghetto mentality of Catholics, eventuated in the decline of parochial schools. As a result, religious orders lost the unique niche they had filled for almost one hundred years in the United States. Finally, Vatican II redefined the vow of poverty with emphasis upon a commitment to issues of social justice and identifying with the materially poor.

Expanding Opportunities for Women

A second major factor, expanding opportunities for women, occurred in the United States at about the same time as Vatican II. By the end of the Council (1965), job opportunities for women were just beginning to open up. By the mid 1970s, when renewal in religious orders was at its peak, increasing numbers of women were entering most professions. Women were no longer limited to teaching and nursing careers. Nuns no longer had to limit their occupational aspirations to teaching in parochial schools. All types of job opportunities were available to them, and nuns took advantage of them. As a result, fewer nuns chose to teach in the remaining parochial schools and thus created a further financial crisis for the schools. Occupational diversity, therefore, not only contributed to the decline in Catholic schools but was also influenced by the fact that religious orders no longer defined parochial school teaching as their primary mission.

Expanding opportunities for women also had a direct effect on both the defection of members from religious orders and the recruitment of new members. Lack of educational and professional opportunities for women was no longer a reason for nuns to remain in their orders. Likewise, entering a religious order was no longer the only viable route to upward mobility for young women. Thus, religious orders had less to offer their members and potential new members.

Credentialism by Professional Associations

A third exogenous factor that lead to structural changes in religious orders was the increased credentialism of personnel demanded by various professional associations as well as encouraged by voices within the Church. In the decade of the 1960s, the National Educational Association and the National Catholic Educational Association began demanding that schools meet certain educational criteria in order to be certified. Primary among these criteria was the professional education of personnel.

Beginning in the 1950s, Pope Pius XII, along with the Sister Formation Movement in this country, began encouraging superiors general to educate their nuns with the credentials necessary for their particular professions. Within a few years, the educational levels of nuns rose substantially.

The demand for professionally credentialed teachers and administrators was one factor that drove up the costs of parochial schools and caused many of them to close. Likewise, the cost of running Catholic hospitals increased with the demands of credentialed personnel. As Catholic schools and hospitals closed, the traditional niche that religious women had filled for a century, was lost.

Declining Birth Rates

A fourth factor, declining birth rates, also affected parochial schools in this country. During the 1940s and 1950s, Catholic schools expanded enormously to provide for the postwar baby boomers. Nuns were in great demand to staff the mushrooming classrooms that were being erected in every parish school in the country. By the end of the 1960s and into the 1970s, the boomers had completed their grammar and high school years, and empty classrooms were widespread. Reduced enrollments also meant reduced tuition to support the schools. As school after school closed its doors, the traditional niche for Catholic nuns disappeared.

Feminist Ideology

The fifth factor that occurred during the 1960s and 1970s in the United States and joined the confluence of exogenous variables affecting religious orders was the feminist movement and feminist ideology that gained many adherents in those decades. With the demise of the cloister and more open boundaries between nuns and the world outside the convent, nuns were exposed to feminist ideas. Many nuns became active feminists, if not in the actual Women's Movement, at least in their thinking. In particular, nuns began challenging the male-hierarchical structure of the Catholic Church, in terms of exclusively male priests, the power of male authorities in Rome to approve the constitutions of religious orders, and the blocked mobility of females in parishes.

Changes in Governmental Regulations and Insurance Companies

Finally, the sixth factor that had an impact on the structural changes in religious orders was change that occurred in federal regulations and insurance companies in the United States. Previously religious orders opted to be tax-exempt institutions, thereby ineligible for social security benefits, but in the early 1970s the federal government gave them the option to pay five years of retroactive social security taxes and become eligible for social security benefits. Many orders took advantage of this option.

Even more important was the increase in liability suits and the expanding role of insurance companies in American society. Because many nuns were involved in high-risk jobs in medical settings and social services, orders were advised to reduce their corporate liability by changing their charter from a member corporation to a memberless one. This change had ramifications for both the legal and financial structures of the order.

The six exogenous factors that occurred at about the same time in the United States produced tremendous structural changes in religious orders of women. Figure 11.1 depicts these structural changes. The three columns indicate the sequence of changes in terms of influences. In the first column are listed those structural changes that were directly affected by the exogenous factors. In the second column are those changes that resulted from the earlier structural changes. The third column presents the two major changes that, ultimately, are leading to the demise of religious orders—anomie of mission and rising median age of members. The arrows between the columns indicate the direction of influence of one factor upon another.

The establishment of a more democratic authority structure had two major consequences. First, members were allowed greater autonomy in choice of occupations as well as work settings; as a result, the occupational diversity among nuns, even those in the same order, expanded. Second, in a democratic authority structure, it is difficult, if not impossible, for administrators to determine the mission and purpose of the group. A more specific set of goals and mission might result in greater solidarity among members and the reestablishment of a niche in society, but given the greater autonomy of members, it is impossible to mandate uniformity of purpose and mission. Members refuse to give up the autonomy and diversity they have experienced in the renewed system.

Likewise, the expansion of job opportunities within Catholic parishes has resulted in greater occupational diversity among nuns. No longer are nuns hired exclusively in the parochial schools; they are now found in various jobs within the parish structure. The expansion of job opportunities in parishes has affected both the defection of nuns as well as the recruitment of new members. Parish employment, not limited to nuns, has expanded to include lay women (and men) as well. Those nuns who want to be involved with parish jobs now have the option to do so as lay women. Some nuns have left their religious orders and continued to work within parish settings. Likewise, joining a religious order is no longer necessary as a requisite for working within Catholic parishes.

The expanding opportunities within parishes is also having an effect upon feminism within religious orders because many nuns who are working within parish settings have come to experience blocked mobility because they are prohibited from ordination and full administration of liturgical functions. Because the top administrator is routinely the pastor and nuns are prohibited from being pastors, they are excluded from upward mobility. Many nuns are leaving parish work because of their frustration with the male-dominated system.

The increased educational level of nuns also affected occupational diversity within religious orders. As nuns became more educated in various fields they chose from a wide range of careers and work settings, many of them outside the parochial structure. This fact influenced the decline of parochial schools because it reduced the pool of low-salaried teachers available to teach in Catholic schools and contributed to their financial crisis. In addition, because of rising retirement costs, religious orders were demanding higher salaries for nun-teachers, a demand that many parishes could not meet.

Occupational diversity also affected the structures of cloister. As nuns began working in various settings, their work demands often included unusual work hours, meetings with a variety of people, the necessity of having a car and budget for professional expenses, continuing education, as well as dress appropriate for their work.

In turn, as nuns left their cloistered environments to be educated in universities, both Catholic and secular, they were exposed to various life-style options that challenged them to reconsider their commitment to a vowed religious life. As education levels rose in religious orders during the late 1960s and into the 1970s defection rates increased.

The loss of a cloistered environment, including shedding uniform dress, increasing association with outsiders, and losing a unique, sacred status within the Church, affected rates of recruitment into religious orders. The costs of celibacy and the forfeiture of married, family life were no longer counterbalanced with the traditional rewards of being a nun.

The shift in meaning of the vow of poverty also affected both occupational diversity of nuns and finances within the orders. With the emphasis upon serving the materially poor and working for rights of the disadvantaged in society, more and more nuns chose to work in poverty programs, providing services for the disadvantaged and working to change social and political structures that discriminated against the poor. Because many of these programs offered low paying salaries for workers, religious orders found themselves subsidizing the salaries of nuns in these jobs. In addition, religious orders became cognizant of their political power in terms of their investments. Rather than investing capital resources in companies that promised the best returns, orders began to investigate company policies in regard to discriminatory practices and social issues such as environmental priorities.

The structural changes that occurred in religious orders of women in the United States as a result of the confluence of external factors resulted in radical changes in three main areas affecting religious orders: occupational diversity, declining rates of recruitment, and increased rates of defection of members. The major impact of occupational diversity among nuns was organizational anomie in regard to the mission and purpose of religious orders. No longer could orders define their mission in terms of teaching, hospital work, and social service. Nuns were involved in all types of work, in both parochial structures and secular society. It is not uncommon today to find nun-lawyers, nun-CPAs, nun-midwives, nun-administrators of companies, nun-board members on all kinds of corporate boards, nun-organizers of poverty programs, and nun-politicians. As religious orders began to articulate their mission for their new constitutions, they found it necessary to frame their mission statements in broad, general terms to encompass these varied works.

In the course of developing broad goal statements, however, religious orders are finding it difficult to ascertain what makes them a unique institution in the Church. Although religious orders today use the term, *corporate mission* to describe the value of membership, at the same time, they struggle to identify the substance of that mission.

The organizational anomie that has resulted from the lack of a definite and specific mission in today's world has affected both defections from religious orders and recruitment of new members. Some nuns have left their orders because they failed to see the unique purpose of religious orders in today's church and society. Likewise, it is difficult for orders to draw new recruits into an organization that lacks clear goals and purpose.

Declining rates of recruitment, along with increased rates of defection especially on the part of younger nuns, have resulted in alarmingly high median ages of members in religious orders today. Without the prospect of member replacement through recruitment, it is virtually impossible for an organization to survive. An increasingly older membership, coupled with uncertainty about the purpose of the institution in modern society, makes the demise of religious orders virtually inevitable.

Organizational Dilemmas

What could religious orders have done to prevent their current demise? Nothing. Given the exogenous factors that came together in the United States at a particular point in history, a series of structural changes were initiated within religious orders that resulted in their loss of mission and high median age of members. Without a unique mission and without the replacement of members, organizational survival is virtually impossible. Religious orders were caught in an organizational dilemma. Once the external factors came together in time and space, the course of change was set in motion. Religious orders had very few degrees of freedom or options. Change was not only inevitable but also mandated by the Church. Given the changes that were taking place on every level of Catholicism, from the Vatican to local parishes, religious orders had to change to be responsive to both their members who were pushing for change and the people whom they were serving in the Church. The refusal to change and adapt to modern life would certainly have resulted in the defection of many members who were attuned to the Council's call for renewal. It would also have been scandalous in a Church that was calling all its members to renewal and adaptation of Church structures.

Paradoxically, however, in the process of renewal religious orders lost both their unique niche in the Church as well as the commitment-building mechanisms that operate to maintain membership. Religious orders were caught in an organizational dilemma.

It was not inevitable that the exogenous factors come together at a particular time and place. Had some of these factors not existed, the prognosis for the future of religious orders in this country may have been different. However, the fact that they did occur set in motion the process that is leading to the demise of the institution in the United States.

Most industrialized nations have also experienced a similar confluence of exogenous factors, such as expanding opportunities for women, a feminist movement, declining birth rates, and demands for credentialing by professional associations, along with Vatican II. As a result, I would predict that the future of religious orders in industrialized countries will follow a course very similar to that of orders in the United States.

However, these same factors do not exist in less industrialized, third world nations where birth rates are still high, the opportunities for women remain limited, the Women's Movement has not been strong, and credentialing of professionals is not required. Although Catholics in these countries were exposed to the renewal demanded by Vatican II, the fact that these other factors were not present leads me to predict that renewal elsewhere did not have the same structural consequences as it did for religious orders in the United States. Without these structural changes, it is highly likely that occupational diversity did not occur; therefore the probability that religious orders in third world countries are experiencing anomie of purpose and mission is diminished. Likewise, in the absence of the structural changes, I predict that neither defection of members was as prevalent nor recruitment of new members as difficult as in industrialized nations. Based on the model of demise presented in this book, I predict that religious orders in third world countries are thriving, much as they were in this country before the mid twentieth century.

Some religious orders in the United States, including my case study order, have provinces or houses in third world countries. I predict that these provinces are flourishing, despite the organizational decline experienced by the mother-order in this country. One scenario of survival for these orders is to focus attention and resources on these provinces, not by recruiting in third world countries and transporting recruits to the United States but by reestablishing the order in a third world country and recruiting indigenous women to remain in their home country.

My prediction for the demise of religious orders is, therefore, limited to the United States and possibly other industrialized nations. It is very possible that religious orders of women, as such, will not disappear from the face of our earth. They may very well continue in nonindustrialized countries, at least until such time as these countries begin to experience the confluence of factors that have led to the demise of religious orders in this country.

As a future research agenda, I am suggesting that the model I present in this book needs to be applied to religious orders cross-nationally. Not only can countries be dichotomized into industrial and nonindustrialized countries for which the exogenous factors vary, but also variations in the presence/absence and degree of these factors needs to be correlated with changes in religious orders.

In addition to cross-national research on religious orders is the issue of how change in religious orders of women compares with what is happening in religious orders of men, as well as the Catholic priesthood in general. Religious orders of brothers, as well as those of ordained priests, are also experiencing decline. The empirical issue of whether organizational decline is following the same pattern as in women's religious orders calls for systematic comparisons. Likewise, comparisons between the demise process in women's orders and the diocesan priest shortage are needed to understand the larger picture of the decline of religious professionals in the Catholic Church.

As I suggested earlier in this chapter, the demise of other types of normative organizations might well follow the same general course as the religious orders discussed in this book. Like religious orders, these organizations depend upon a clear articulation of their mission in society and a membership that is viable in terms of age distribution. If their mission loses its focus and members are not replaced through recruitment, then the demise of the organization is inevitable.

Again, exogenous factors can coalesce in time and place to produce loss of purpose, defections, and lack of recruitment. In terms of normative organizations, four possible types of exogenous factors are likely to lead to structural changes and the eventual demise of the organization. First, organizations might experience goal fulfillment and lose their reason for existing. Second, their goal might become irrelevant in a changing society. Third, organizations can lose their resource base and be unable to survive. Finally, organizational competition might mean that other organizations take over the functions of the organization, which makes survival unnecessary.

To determine the generalizability of the demise model presented in this book, further research on various value-focused organizations is needed. Both exogenous and structural change variables must be identified in terms of their effects upon goals and membership demographics. Only then can the probability of the demise of these organizations be predicted.

Given the structural changes in religious orders that were initiated by the confluence of exogenous factors in the United States in the middle of this century, the demise of religious orders in this country seems highly likely. The challenge for these orders is the nature of the legacy they will leave as they confront the reality that they are becoming a vanishing institution in our society.

References

Abbott, Walter M., ed. 1966. *The Documents of Vatican II*. New York: America Press.

Akers, R., and F.C. Campbell. 1970. Size and the administrative component in occupational avocation. *Pacific Sociological Review* 13: 241–251.

Aldrich, Howard E. 1979. *Organizations and Environments*. Englewood Cliffs, N.J.: Prentice-Hall.

Anderson, Karen. 1988. A history of women's work in the United States. In *Women Working: Theories and Facts in Perspective*, ed. Ann Hilton Stromberg and Shirley Harkers, 25–41. Mountain View, Calif.: Mayfield Publishing Company.

Arbuckle, Gerald A. 1988. *Out of Chaos: Refounding Religious Congregations*. New York: Paulist Press.

Argenti, J. 1976. *Corporate Collapse*. New York: Halstead Press.

Behn, R. 1978. Closing a government facility. *Public Administration Review* 38: 332–338.

———. 1982. The fundamentals of cutback management. In *What Role for Government: Lessons from Policy Research*, ed. R. Zerkhauser and D. Leebaert, 310–322. Durham, N.C.: Duke University Press.

Benson, J.K. 1975. The interorganizational network as a political economy. *Administrative Science Quarterly* 20: 229–249.

Bozeman, B., and E. A. Slusher. 1979. Security and environmental stress in public organizations: A conjectural essay. Working paper. Maxwell School, Syracuse University.

Bromley, D.G., and B.C. Busching. 1988. Understanding the structure of contractual and covenental social relations: Implications for the sociology of religion. *Sociological Analysis*. 49: 15–32.

Byrne, Patricia. 1990. *Transforming Parish Ministry: Changing Roles of Catholic Clergy, Laity and Women Religious, 1930–1980*. New York: Crossroads.

Cada, Lawrence, S.M., Raymond Fitz, S.M., Thomas Giardino, S.M., and Carol Lichtenberg, S.N.D. 1979. *Shaping the Coming Age of Religious Life*. New York: Seabury Press.

Cameron, K.S. 1983. Strategic responses to the conditions of decline: Higher education and the private sector. *Journal of Higher Education* 54: 359–380.

Cameron, Kim S., Robert I. Sutton and David A. Whetten. 1988. Issues in organizational decline. In *Readings in Organizational Decline: Frameworks, Research and Prescriptions,* ed. Cameron, Sutton and Whetten. Cambridge, Mass: Ballenger Publishing Co.

Cameron, Kim S., and D.O. Ulrich. 1986. Transformational leadership in colleges and universities. In *Higher Education Handbook of Theory and Research,* Vol. 3, ed. John M. Smart. New York: Agathon.

Cameron, Kim S., and Raymond F. Zammute. 1983. Matching managerial strategies to conditions of decline. *Human Resource Management,* Vol. 22. New York: John Wylie and Sons.

Campbell, Joseph. 1968. *The Masks of God: Creative Mythology.* New York: Viking Press.

———. 1988. *The Power of Myth.* New York: Doubleday.

Carden, Maren L. 1969. *Oneida: Utopian Community to Modern Corporation.* Baltimore: Johns Hopkins University Press.

Carpenter, Teresa. 1980. Courage and pain: Women who love God and defy their churches. *Redbook* (April): 19, 49–56.

Coleman, James S., and Thomas Hoffer. 1987. *Public and Private Schools: The Impact of Communities.* New York: Basic Books.

Cornfield, D.B. 1983. Chances of layoff in a corporation: A case study. *Administrative Science Quarterly* 28: 503–520.

Cyert, R. M., and J. G. March. 1963. *A Behavioral Theory of the Firm.* Englewood Cliffs, N.J.: Prentice-Hall.

Dahrendorf, R. 1959. *Class and Class Conflict in Industrial Society.* Stanford: Stanford University Press.

Dolan, J. P. 1985. *The American Catholic Experience.* Garden City, New York: Image Books.

Dopfner, Cardinal Julius. 1969. *La Documentation Catholique* 66 (Sept. 7): 789.

Dulles, Avery. 1988. *The Reshaping of Catholicism: Current Challenges in the Theology of Church.* New York: Harper & Row.

Ebaugh, Helen Rose Fuchs. 1977. *Out of the Cloister: A Study of Organizational Dilemmas.* Austin: The University of Texas Press.

———. 1978. Catholic nuns: Unwitting feminists. Paper presented at the Southwest Social Science Meeting. March, Dallas, Texas.

———. 1980. *Becoming an Ex: The Process of Role Exiting.* Chicago: University of Chicago Press.

———. 1984. Leaving the convent: The experience of public exit and self-transformation. In *The Existential Self in Society,* ed. Joseph A. Kotarba and Andrea Fontana. Chicago: University of Chicago Press.

———. 1991. The revitalization movement in the Catholic Church: The Institutional dilemma of power. *Sociological Analysis* 52, 1: 1–12.

Etzioni, Amitai. 1961. *A Comparative Analysis of Complex Organizations.* New York: Free Press.

Festinger, Leon, Henry W. Riecken, and Stanley Schachter. 1956. *When Prophecy Fails.* Minneapolis: University of Minnesota Press.

Fichter, Joseph. 1988. *A Sociologist Looks at Religion.* Wilmington, Del.: Michael Glazier.

Fox, Zenobia V. 1986. A post-Vatican II phenomenon: Lay ministries. Ph.D. diss., Fordham University.

Freeman, J., and M.T. Hannan. 1975. Growth and decline processes in organizations. *American Sociological Review* 40: 215–228.

Friedan, Betty. 1975. Review printed in the jacket of *The Courage to Choose: An American Nun's Story,* by Mary Griffin. Boston: Little, Brown and Company.

Goffman, Erving. 1961. *Asylums.* Garden City, New York: Doubleday.

Goldner, Fred H., R. Richard Ritti, and Thomas P. Ference. 1977. The production of cynical knowledge in organizations. *American Sociological Review* 42: 539–551.

Gollin, Gillian Lindt. 1967. *Moravians in Two Worlds: A Study of Changing Communities.* New York: Columbia University Press.

Greeley, Andrew M. 1990. *The Catholic Myth: The Behavior and Beliefs of American Catholics.* New York: Charles Scribner's Sons.

Greenhalgh, L. 1978. A cost-benefit balance sheet for evaluating layoffs or a policy strategy. Ithaca: New York State School of Industrial and Labor Relations.

————. 1983. Organizational decline. *Research and the Sociology of Organizations* 2: 231–276.

Greenhalgh, L., and T.D. Jick. 1978. The relocation of a rural hospital unit: The impact of rumor and ambiguity on employees. Ithaca: New York State School of Industrial and Labor Relations.

Greenhalgh, L., and Z. Rosenblatt. 1984. Job insecurity: Toward conceptual clarity. *Academic Management Review* 9: 434–438.

Griffin, Mary. 1975. *The Courage to Choose: An American Nun's Story.* Boston: Little, Brown and Company.

Hall, D. T., and R. Mansfield. 1971. Organizational and individual response to external stress. *Administrative Science Quarterly* 16: 533–547.

Hall, R. I. 1976. A system pathology of an organization: The rise and fall of the old "Saturday Evening Post." *Administrative Science Quarterly* 21:185–211.

Hannan, Michael T., and John Freeman. 1989. *Organizational Ecology.* Cambridge: Harvard University Press.

Hennesey, James. 1981. *American Catholics: A History of the Roman Catholic Community in the United States.* New York: Oxford University Press.

Heslin, Julie A. 1983. In transition: A study of religious administrators in nontraditional roles. Ph.D. diss. Fordham University.

Hirschman, Albert O. 1970. *Exit, Voice and Loyalty: Responses to Decline in Firms, Organizations, and States.* Cambridge: Harvard University Press.

Hirshhorn, Larry and Associates. 1983. *Cutting Back: Retrenchment and Redevelopment in Human and Community Services.* San Francisco: Jossey-Bass Publishers.

Joseph, S.M., et al. 1980. *New Ministries of Woman Religious: Role Conflict and Coping Styles.* Chicago: Religious Formation Center.

Kanter, Rosabeth Moss. 1972. *Commitment and Community: Communes and Utopias in Sociological Perspective.* Cambridge: Harvard University Press.

Kanter, Rosabeth Moss, and Barry A. Stein, eds. 1979. *Life in Organizations: Workplaces as People Experience Them.* New York: Basic Books

Kimberly, John R., Robert H. Miles, and Associates. 1980. *The Organizational Life Cycle: Issues in the Creation, Transformation and Decline of Organizations.* Washington, D.C.: Jossey-Bass Publishers.

Kolarska, L., and H. Aldrich. 1980. Exit, voice and silence: Consumers' and managers' responses to organizational decline. *Organizational Studies* 1, 1: 41–58.

Kolmer, Elizabeth. 1984. *Religious Women in the U.S.* Wilmington, Del.: Michael Glazier.

LaMagdeleine, Donald R. 1986. U.S. Catholic Church-related jobs as dual labor markets: A speculative inquiry. *Review of Religious Research* 27: 315–327.

Levine, C. H. 1978. Organizational decline and Catholic management. *Public Administration Review* 38: 316–325.

———. 1979. More on cutback management: Hard questions for hard times. *Public Administration Review* 39: 179–183.

Lifton, Jay. 1961. *Thought Reform and the Psychology of Totalism.* New York: Norton.

Loving, Rush, Jr. 1979. W. T. Grant's last days—as seen from store 1192. In *Life in Organizations and Workplaces as People Experience Them,* ed. Kanter and Stein. New York: Basic Books.

Meyer, Marshall W., and Lynne Zucker. 1989. *Permanently Failing Organizations.* London: Sage Publications.

Meyers, Sr. Bertrand. 1965. *Sisters for the Twenty-First Century.* New York: Sheed and Ward.

Michels, Robert. 1949. *Political Parties.* Transl. by Edward Cedar Paul. Glencoe, Ill.: Free Press.

National Catholic Reporter. 1982. (August 13): 11.

Neal, Marie Augusta. 1970. The relationship between religious belief and structural change in religious orders: Developing an effective measuring instrument. *Review of Religious Research* Part I: 12 (Fall): 2–16.

———. 1971. The relationship between religious belief and structural change in religious orders: Some evidence. *Review of Religious Research,* Part II: 12 (Spring): 153–164.

———. 1981. The Sisters' Survey, 1980: A Report. *National Association of Women Religious* 10 (May–June): No. 5.

———. 1984. *Catholic Sisters in Transition: From the 1960's to the 1980's.* Wilmington, Del.: Michael Glazier.

———. 1990. *From Nuns to Sisters: An Expanding Vocation.* Mystic, Conn.: Twenty-Third Publications.

New York Times. 1984 (Feb. 25): 46.

Quinonez, Lora Ann, C.D.P., and Mary Daniel Turner, SNDdeN. 1992. *The Transformation of American Catholic Sisters.* Philadelphia: Temple University Press.

Ritzer, George, and David Walczak. 1986. *Working: Conflict and Change.* 3rd ed. Englewood Cliffs, N.J.: Prentice-Hall.

Rynne, Xavier. 1968. *Vatican Council II.* New York: Farrar Strauss & Giroux.

Salaman, Graeme. 1981. *Work Organization and Class Structure.* Armonk, N.Y.: M. E. Sharpe.

San Giovanni, Lucinda. 1978. *Ex-Nuns: A Study of Emergent Role Passage.* Norwood, N. J.: Ablex Publishing Corporation.

Schneiders, Sandra Marie, I.H.M. 1986. *New Wineskins: Re-Imaging Religious Life Today.* New York: Paulist Press.

———. 1987. Reflections on the history of religious life and contemporary developments. In *Turning Points in Religious Life,* ed. Carol Tingley, I.H.M. Wilmington, Del.: Michael Glazier.

Schoenherr, Richard A., and Annemette Sorensen. 1982. Social change in religious organizations: Consequences of the clergy decline in the U.S. Catholic Church. *Sociological Analysis* 43: 52–71.

Schuler, R. S. 1980. Definition and conceptualization of stress in organizations. *Organizational Behavior and Human Performance* 25: 184–215.

Scott, W. Richard. 1981. *Organizations: Rational, Natural and Open Systems.* Englewood Cliffs, N.J.: Prentice-Hall.

Seidler, John, and Katherine Meyer. 1989. *Conflict and Change in the Catholic Church.* New Brunswick, N.J.: Rutgers University Press.

Sherif, M., and C. Sherif. 1953. *Groups in Harmony and Tension.* New York: Harper & Row.

Sills, David L. 1957. *The Volunteers: Means and Ends in a National Organization.* Glencoe, Ill.: Free Press.

Slote, Alfred. 1969. *Termination: The Closing at the Baker Plant.* Indianapolis: Bobbs-Merrill.

Smart, C., and I. Vertinsky. 1977. Design for crisis decision units. *Administrative Science Quarterly* 22: 640–657.

Sorel, Georges. 1941. *Reflections on Violence.* Trans. by T. E. Hulme. New York: Peter Smith Publications.

Staw, Barry M., Lance E. Sandelandir, and Jane E. Dutton. 1981. Threat-rigidity effects in organizational behavior: A multilevel analysis. *Administrative Science Quarterly* 26: 501–524.

Stein, Barry. 1979. Organizations in trouble: Two vignettes. In *Life in Organizations: Workplaces as People Experience Them.* New York: Basic Books.

Sutton, Robert I. 1984. Managing organizational death. *Human Resource Management* 22: 377–390. New York: John Wiley.

Sweeney, William. 1980. *Roman Catholicism: The Search for Relevance.* New York: St. Martin's Press.

Thompson, Margaret. 1986. Discovering foremothers: Sisters, society, and the American Catholic experience. *U.S. Catholic Historian* 5 (3 and 4 Nov.): 273–290.

Tobin, Mary Luke. 1967. The mission of the religious in the twentieth century. In *Vows but No Walls: An Analysis of Religious Life,* ed. Eugene E. Grollsnec, S.J. St. Louis: B. Herder Book.

Tsouderos, J. E. 1955. Organizational change in terms of a series of selected variables. *American Sociological Review* 20: 206–210.

U.S. Bureau of the Census. 1975. Historical statistics of the United States: Colonial times to 1970, Part I: 131–132.

U.S. Department of Labor, Bureau of Labor Statistics. 1986. Employment and earnings (Jan.).

Wallace, Ruth. 1992. *They Call Her Pastor.* New York: State University of New York Press.

Weaver, Mary Jo. 1986. Inside outsiders: Sisters and the women's movement. In *New Catholic Women: A Contemporary Challenge to Traditional Religious Authority,* chap. 3. San Francisco: Harper & Row.

Wenzel, Kristan. 1990. The impact of religiousness on retirement expectations among women religious in the United States. Unpublished paper presented at the 1990 meeting of the Eastern Sociological Society, Boston.

Whetten, D. A. 1980a. Organizational decline: A neglected topic in organizational science. *Academy of Management Review* 5:577–588.

———. 1980b. Sources, responses and effects of organizational decline. In *The Organizational Life Cycle,* ed. J. R. Kimberly and R. H. Miles. San Francisco: Jossey-Bass.

———. 1981. Organizational responses to scarcity: Exploring the obstacles to innovative approaches to retrenchment in education. *Education Administrative Quarterly* 17: 80–97.

———. 1987. Organizational growth and decline processes. *Annual Review of Sociology* 13: 335–358.

Wittberg, Patricia. 1985. Transformations in religious commitments. *Review for Religions* 27: 161–170.

———. 1988. Outward orientation in declining organizations. In *Claiming Our Truth: Reflections and Identity by United States Women Religious,* ed. Nadine Foley. Washington, D.C.: Leadership Conference of Women Religious.

———. 1989. The dual labor market in the Catholic Church: Expanding a speculative inquiry. *Review of Religious Research* 30: 287–290.

———. 1989. Nonordained workers in the Catholic Church: Power and mobility among American nuns. *Journal for the Scientific Study of Religion* 28, 2: 148–161.

———. 1991. *Creating a Future for Religious Life: A Sociological Perspective.* New York: Paulist Press.

Wood, James R. 1981. *Leadership in Voluntary Organizations.* New Brunswick, N.J.: Rutgers University Press.

Wynne, George. 1983. *Cutback Management: A Trinational Perspective.* New Brunswick, N.J.: Transaction Books.

Yetten, P. W. 1975. Leadership style in stressful and nonstressful situations. In *Management Stress,* ed. Gowler and K. Legge. New York: John Wiley.

Zablocki, Benjamin. 1980. *Alienation and Charisma: Contemporary American Communes.* Glenco, Ill.: Free Press.

Author Index

Subject Index

Alter, Karl, 139
American Catholic Church, 80, 143
apostolic orders, 17, 19, 21; age of,
    12 fig., 16–17, 18
Aquinas, Thomas, 112
Arthur Andersen and Company, 125,
    132
asceticism, 11–12, 13, 17
aspirancies, 96–97
associate programs, 38–39, 45, 94; in
    the Sisters of Service, 103–105,
    110, 151
Augustinians, 15
authority structure: in the Catholic
    Church, 146, 162, 164 (*see also*
    Roman Catholic Church: male
    domination of); pre-Vatican II, 49,
    61–62, 65–67; in religious orders,
    8, 20–21, 23, 31–32, 37–38, 44–
    45, 52, 60, 77, 78, 83, 111, 159,
    164, 165, 168; in the Sisters of
    Service, 57, 59, 60, 69–71, 72–77,
    108

baby boomers, 82, 84, 167
Beguines, 15
Benedict, Saint, 12–13
birth rate, 96, 172; and the decline of
    Catholic schools, 86, 167; and the
    demise of religious orders, 162,
    163 fig., 167
Bruno, Saint, 14

Camaldolese monastery of Italy, 14
Carthusians, 14
Caspary, Sister Anita, 140
Catholic Action, 66
Catholic Church. *See* Roman
    Catholic Church
Catholics: number of, in U.S., 80

celibacy, 26, 28, 137, 155; costs of,
    95, 96, 106, 170; post-Vatican II,
    24, 25; pre-Vatican II, 12, 17, 19,
    20, 25; as reason for defection, 38,
    111, 128
Chavez, Cesar, 145
Chevron Oil Company, 120
Christian Education of Youth, The
    (Pius XI), 19
Chrysler Corporation, 39, 40
CICL. *See* Congregation for
    Religious Institutes of Conse-
    crated Life
Cistercian monastery at La Trappe, 14
civil rights movement, 71, 84, 144,
    159
Citeaux, 14
cloister, 3, 5, 12; demise of, 26, 27,
    29, 96, 133, 160, 164, 165, 167;
    post-Vatican II, 21, 22–23, 24, 25,
    26–27, 110, 139, 169; pre-Vatican
    II, 14, 17, 18, 25, 26–27, 61, 90,
    110
CMSW. *See* Conference of Major
    Superiors of Religious Congrega-
    tions of Women
cognitive dissonance, 38
communes, 6, 130–131, 161. *See also*
    intentional communities
Conference of Major Superiors of
    Religious Congregations of
    Women (CMSW), 19, 47, 71, 72,
    85, 124. *See also* Leadership
    Conference of Women Religious
Congregation for Religious Institutes
    of Consecrated Life (CICL), 5,
    147
Congregation of Service, Inc. *See*
    Sisters of Service: as corporate
    voluntary mission

185